Planned Giving Workbook

Also by Ronald R. Jordan and Katelyn L. Quynn:

Planned Giving, Second Edition: Management, Marketing, and Law
(ISBN 0-471-35102-4)

Invest in Charity: A Donor's Guide to Charitable Giving
(ISBN 0-471-41439-5)

Planned Giving for Small Nonprofits
(ISBN 0-471-21209-1)

Planned Giving Workbook

RONALD R. JORDAN
KATELYN L. QUYNN

John Wiley & Sons, Inc.

ISBN: 0-471-21211-3
Printed in the United States of America
10 9 8 7 6 5 4 3 2 1

About the Authors

Ronald R. Jordan is the former Assistant Vice President of University Advancement and former Director of New Mexico State University's planned giving program. He has been a member of the bar since 1975 and is a graduate of the New England School of Law. As an assistant professor at the university, he teaches courses on financial planning and consumer electronics. Previously, he taught courses in federal income taxation and estate planning. Jordan is the former Director of Planned Giving at Boston University. He also consults with nonprofit organizations.

Katelyn L. Quynn is Director of Development for Massachusetts General Hospital's planned and major gift program, and Director of Planned Giving for Partners Healthcare System. She was named Planned Giving Professional of the Year in 1996, is a past President of The Planned Giving Group of New England, and former board member of the National Committee on Planned Giving. She graduated from Tufts University and Boston University School of Law.

About the CD-ROM

INTRODUCTION

The forms on the enclosed CD-ROM are saved in Microsoft Word for Windows version 7.0. In order to use the forms, you will need to have word processing software capable of reading Microsoft Word for Windows version 7.0 files.

SYSTEM REQUIREMENTS

- IBM PC or compatible computer
- CD-ROM drive
- Windows 95 or later
- Microsoft Word for Windows version 7.0 (including the Microsoft converter*) or later or other word processing software capable of reading Microsoft Word for Windows 7.0 files.

    *Word 7.0 needs the Microsoft converter file installed in order to view and edit all enclosed files. If you have trouble viewing the files, download the free converter from the Microsoft web site. The URL for the converter is: *http://office.microsoft.com/downloads/2000/wrd97cnv.aspx*

    Microsoft also has a viewer that can be downloaded, which allows you to view, but not edit documents. This viewer can be downloaded at: *http://office.microsoft.com/downloads/9798/wdvw9716.aspx*

    NOTE: Many popular word processing programs are capable of reading Microsoft Word for Windows 7.0 files. However, users should be aware that a slight amount of formatting might be lost when using a program other than Microsoft Word.

USING THE FILES

Loading Files

To use the files, launch your word processing program. Select **File, Open** from the pull-down menu. Select the appropriate drive and directory. A list of files should appear. If you do not see a list of files in the directory, you need to select **WORD DOCUMENT (*.DOC)** under **Files of Type.** Double click on the file you want to open. Edit the file according to your needs.

Printing Files

If you want to print the files, select **File, Print** from the pull-down menu.

Saving Files

When you have finished editing a file, you should save it under a new file name by selecting **File, Save As** from the pull-down menu.

User Assistance

If you need assistance with installation or if you have a damaged disk, please contact Wiley Technical Support at:

Phone: (201) 748-6753
Fax: (201) 748-6450 (Attention: Wiley Technical Support)
Email: *techhelp@wiley.com*
URL: *www.wiley.com/techsupport*

To place additional orders or to request information about other Wiley products, please call (800) 225-5945.

Contents

Preface

The *Planned Giving Workbook* provides nonprofit organizations of all types and sizes with a comprehensive collection of working documents used in planned giving. These documents have been designed and perfected by the authors during their more than 40 years (combined) experience. Planned giving and development staff members spend a considerable amount of time writing documents to a variety of audiences. The writing takes many forms including correspondence, marketing materials, proposals, and exhibits. Well-written documents attract donors and deliver the nonprofit's message. The *Workbook* provides advice to the reader on how to modify and maximize the use of these documents.

Like all forms, these documents illustrate one way to present information. Each must be customized to meet the needs of the donor and the nonprofit organization. This customization can be done easily using a Find and Replace tool of a word processing program. Please remember that all documents that contain planned giving calculations must be updated to reflect current discount and annuity rates and current tax laws that change regularly. Readers should update the calculations with their own planned giving software to recalculate payout rates, charitable income tax deductions, and other financial data. Before use, all forms should be reviewed and approved by the nonprofit organization's legal counsel to make certain that they comply with local law and practice and that they are appropriate and compatible with the nonprofit's mission and objectives. The *Workbook* and accompanying CD-ROM contain 425 documents that are divided into seven categories:

1. Marketing materials
2. Agreements
3. Correspondence
4. Administrative documents
5. Exhibits
6. Presentations
7. IRS forms and tax-related documents

Acknowledgments

Writing a book takes teamwork, cooperation, and the participation of a number of individuals, each of whom makes valuable contributions to the manuscript and text. The authors wish to thank the following individuals for their help in the production of this manuscript.

- **Don Beasley, CPA, Beasley, Mitchell and Company, Las Cruces, New Mexico.** Don reviewed the technical chapters in this book and made significant contributions in improving its integrity and in making a difficult subject more understandable. Don is a skilled practitioner who appreciates the impact that planned giving has on a donor and a charity.

- **Stephen A. Bernhaardt, Ph.D., holder of the Andrew B. Kirkpatrick Chair in Writing, University of Delaware, Department of English.** The authors wish to thank Steve who coauthored the Introduction to the *Planned Giving Workbook*. The Introduction is a guide to improving one's writing and a guide to writing effective planned giving and development documents. Steve is a fine writer and a great teacher. Steve understands the importance of writing in the workplace and we are grateful to him for sharing his expertise with our readers.

- **Dianne C. Jordan.** The authors wish to thank Ron's wife, Dianne, for her work as a production assistant in the development of the manuscript. The authors are indebted to her for her generous contribution of time and energy.

- **Diana Maria Garcia, Las Cruces, New Mexico.** Diana has worked with Ron Jordan for almost 11 years. As a volunteer, Diana has been involved in many aspects of this book, and the authors thank her for her able assistance and dedication.

- **PG Calc, 129 Mount Auburn Street, Cambridge, Massachusetts, 617-497-4970,** *www.pgcalc.com.* The authors wish to thank PG Calc and its fine staff for their generosity in allowing us to reprint PG Calc calculations and for creating such a wonderful product.

- **Our families.** The authors thank their families—Dianne C. Jordan and Derek Jordan and Barry, Henry, and Andrew Smith—for giving us the time to develop and write this book.
- **John Wiley & Sons, Inc.** As usual, it is always a pleasure to do business with the staff of John Wiley & Sons.
- Last, we thank our employers and our donors, who provide opportunities for us to learn our craft.

We hope that the *Planned Giving Workbook* with CD-ROM exceeds your expectations. We invite your suggestions and welcome your comments.

RONALD R. JORDAN
KATELYN L. QUYNN

July 2002

Introduction to the
Planned Giving Workbook

For planned giving officers and development staff members, developing documents is an important part of the job. Nonprofit employees must develop documents that take many forms, including the drafting of detailed proposals describing complicated gift options; marketing materials; correspondence to donors, professional advisors, and staff members; exhibits; agreements; presentation materials; and Internal Revenue Service (IRS) and tax-related documents. This chapter, together with the other materials in this workbook, will help employees of development organizations draft, design, and develop a variety of documents that can accomplish their organizations' goals.

Documents serve many purposes. They attract donors and prospects, help to deliver the nonprofit organization's message, and present charitable gift options in a professional manner. Documents also can enhance the image of the planned giving office and influence the public's perception of the nonprofit organization. Most important, thoughtful and well-written documents help to sustain and nurture relationships over time with those donors who share common goals with the nonprofit organization.

This chapter provides an organizational overview of the types of documents contained in the *Planned Giving Workbook* and in the accompanying CD-ROM. In addition, it discusses the issues that readers should consider while preparing documents, and it provides suggestions for developing good writing practices within the organization.

The *Planned Giving Workbook* contains a CD-ROM with 425 documents to assist nonprofit development staff, mentors, and planned giving officers in their jobs. These documents serve as models, or templates, to be used in planned giving and development. The CD-ROM contains a wide variety of representative and illustrative documents that are used in a planned giving or development program. Although it is not

This chapter has been coauthored by Stephen A. Bernhardt, Ph.D., holder of the Andrew B. Kirkpatrick Chair in Writing, University of Delaware, Department of English. He is coauthor with Edward L. Smith of *Writing at Work: Professional Skills for People on the Job* (NTC Publishing Group: Lincolnwood, Illinois).

possible to include every document used in a planned giving program, these documents represent those likely to be used regularly and frequently. The documents are divided into seven categories, and the *Workbook* devotes a chapter to each type of document. The seven categories are:

1. Marketing
2. Agreements
3. Correspondence
4. Administrative documents
5. Exhibits
6. Presentations
7. Tax and IRS documents

The following section defines and exemplifies each category.

TYPES OF DOCUMENTS

Planned giving officers prepare many types of documents for a variety of purposes. The seven types of documents and purposes are listed in Exhibit I-1.

EXHIBIT I-1.   DOCUMENT DESCRIPTIONS

Type of Document	Purpose
1. Marketing Documents	Communicate information to groups about charitable gifts to donors, prospects, and other constituents
Newsletters	Educate potential prospects about giving opportunities
Planned Giving Advertisements	Inform the public about the nonprofit organization and its services
Buckslips	Advertise a particular program with a focused informational piece of literature
Columns	Describe specific programs and gift opportunities through newsletters
Brochures	Educate the general public about detailed gift options, funding opportunities, and a broad array of named funds
Guides	Describe in a booklet the gift options, showing how planned gifts can provide financial benefits to the donor
Prospect Letters	Seek new relationships and cultivate existing ones
2. Agreements	Govern the use, scope, and purpose of a donor's gift
Endowed Funds	Govern the use of funds transferred to establish a permanent endowed fund

---

EXHIBIT I-1.   DOCUMENT DESCRIPTIONS *(Continued)*

Type of Document	Purpose
Current-Use Awards	Govern a donor's gift for immediate use
Specific Purpose Funds	Create chairs, professorships, or other specific funds
Other	Agreements that pertain to real estate gifts, tangible personal property, and other noncash assets
3. **Administrative Documents**	Administer the planned giving staff and manage the organization's contacts
Office Management	Assist in the administration of the office
Donor Management	Manage donors and prospects using special tools
4. **Correspondence**	Communicate, educate, and build relationships with individual donors
Donor Letters	Inform about planned gifts and the organization's accomplishments, cultivate relations
Prospect Letters	Renew relationships, cultivate existing ones
Professional Advisor Letters	Share information on charitable gift planning
Nonprofit Staff Member Letters, Memos, and Minutes	Educate internally about gift options and donor strategies
5. **Exhibits**	Teach and inform others through examples about the work of the organization
Estate Planning Documents	Attract donors, prospects, and staff
Materials for Workshops/Seminars	Educate faculty, staff, volunteers, and potential donors
Numerical and Data-Based Documents	Demonstrate mathematical results and data trends
Agendas	Organize events, meetings, and workshops
6. **Presentations**	Educate others through speaking about planned giving programs
Planned Giving Presentation	Information about planned giving, life income gifts, gifts of assets other than cash, estate and tax planning
Presentation Thumbnail	Contains the same information as Planned Giving Presentation but in an outline format
7. **Tax and IRS Documents**	Meet tax requirements through a series of forms
Charitable Remainder Unitrusts	IRS-approved unitrust forms
Charitable Remainder Annuity Trusts	IRS-approved annuity trust forms
Pooled Income Funds	Pooled income fund documents

Each type of document performs some purpose for the organization. Notice that each purpose statement in Exhibit I-1 begins with an *active verb*. In planning giving, donors *make* gifts, *transfer* stock, *support* nonprofits, and *write* checks. The verbs represent the action that shapes each document. Producing documents is all about doing something—accomplishing the work of the nonprofit organization.

In planned giving, the purpose of the document is often to explain the benefits of a specific gift option or to compare different gift options. Many of the documents are educational in nature. They are designed to educate donors, prospects, and professional advisors about the tax consequences and life income benefits of planned gifts. They also are designed to sustain and develop the relationship between the donor and the charity.

When drafting a document, think first about purpose. Writers who are clear about the purpose have a much better chance of writing an effective document.

COMMUNICATE A MESSAGE FOR A PURPOSE

Documents must communicate information clearly and precisely to fulfill their purposes. The document's purpose drives all communication. Ask:

- What is the purpose of this planned giving document?
- What do I (the writer) hope to accomplish? What is the intended outcome from this communication?
- What are the purposes of my audience? Why should donors want to work with the nonprofit and support the work of the organization?

KNOW THE AUDIENCE AND BE RESPONSIVE TO IT

Development documents are powerful tools that carry the nonprofit organization's message to all of its constituents. Often the written message reaches donors and prospects in their homes and offices, places where the planned giving officer cannot yet enter. The message creates the opportunity for a dialogue between the nonprofit organization and its constituents. Introductory letters establish the beginning of a relationship that, it is hoped, will continue over time, to the mutual benefit of both the donor and the nonprofit organization. Subsequent documents nurture relationships, helping those relationships grow and become more meaningful over time.

Instead of thinking about what the writer needs to tell the reader (self-centered thinking), think about the readers—who they are, what they want, what motivates them, what fulfills their goals (audience-centered thinking). Depending on the nonprofit organization, the reader could be an alumnus, a grateful patient, a patron, a volunteer, a vice president, a faculty member, a professional advisor, or a board member. Each reader must be treated individually; he or she must be allowed to influence the tone and style of the document. When preparing to write, conjure up an image of the audience—think of specific people who come to mind. Imagine how they will respond to written communication. Talk to them inside your head. Argue with them and persuade them to consider your point of view.

Unsuccessful speakers, like unsuccessful writers, fail to consider the audience. Consider these questions:

- Who is the audience?
- What goals does the nonprofit share with potential donors? What does the reader want to achieve? (audience purpose)
- What is the audience's level of knowledge and experience?
- What does the audience *need* to know? What would they really *like* to know?
- What is the existing relationship between the nonprofit and the audience? What future relationship should be built?

Thinking through purpose and audience should help the writer formulate a strategy for written communication. The writer should be able to nutshell (put in a very succinct statement) the purpose and define the intended audience. The writer should be able to state clear facts about the audience that can be used to shape the document. Thinking clearly about the purpose of the writing and the intended audience forms the basis for effective communication and strong documents. Exhibit I-2 poses questions that may help to focus the writer.

EXHIBIT I-2.   WORKSHEET: NUTSHELL YOUR DOCUMENT

- What is the purpose of the writing?

  _____

- Who is the audience?

  _____

- What does the audience need to know?

  _____

- How well do you know the audience?

  _____

- What is the nature of the document?

  _____

- What is the audience's goal?

  _____

- What is your goal?

  _____

Use Outlining

Properly organized documents are usually first outlined. An outline allows the writer to plan the document much in the same way an architect draws a blueprint. Outlining allows the writer to divide the document into smaller, more manageable units. Long, detailed letters with lots of information must be outlined; otherwise the letters will likely confuse the readers. In addition, proposals, complicated gift documents, and marketing materials like brochures, newsletters, and columns should all be outlined. Outlining may seem to slow the pace, but in the long run, it improves efficiency and boosts productivity.

When preparing the outline, think about what must be covered and about the order in which information should be presented. In most professional writing, the writer should be prepared to state the purpose right from the start—to deliver the *Bottom Line Up Front* (BLUF). One cannot fool readers or lull them into simply agreeing with one or acting in a prescribed manner. Readers are suspicious of correspondence until they know who is writing, for what purpose, with what intended result. The writer might as well state clearly the reason for the writing, what the issues are, and why that particular audience is being addressed. When asking for financial support, do not risk alienating the audience by playing coy.

When outlining the introductory paragraph, think about what should be accomplished. In most cases, if the writer wants the audience to *do* something, come right out and say so. Be open about the purpose because the mission and project goals are shared with the audience—the writer is presenting an opportunity to work together on something important. Do not be blunt but do be honest, direct, and open in the approach.

When organizing the body of the document, build on what the audience already knows and then extend their knowledge. This is a basic principle of moving from known or shared information to new or unknown information. In the outline, be prepared to plan for some context or background information—stating what the writer and the reader already understand because of past dealings—before offering information on new developments, new initiatives, new accomplishments.

Outline the major points and support each with examples, a brief story, some facts and figures, or a small surprise. At the top level of the outline, the writer should place the main points that he or she wants the reader to understand. If possible, tie these points to actions. At the lower levels of the outline should be those nuggets that carry the day, that drive the point home. Each major paragraph or section should be like a sandwich, with the more general statements or actions at the beginning and end and the supporting material in the middle. One test of a good outline is to read just the sentences at the top level of the document (the first sentence of each paragraph, or the first and last sentence of each paragraph), and see if the sequence of topics or generalizations makes a compelling and coherent argument on its own.

When completing the outline, think strategically about how to close the communication. What specifically will the closing ask for? How will the point be driven home? What is the take-home message for the audience? What do you want them to do as they finish reading? The close of a business document is frequently "next steps," suggesting how to move forward from the current position. Be clear about the proposed next steps.

When outlining, do not get hung up on format. Develop an outline strategy that is productive, not one that the writer imagines is the "correct way" to outline. The outline is a place to think and develop a strategy. It should put into place your prior thinking about purpose and audience. It should map a sequence of discussion and frame a coherent document. Time spent writing an outline will pay dividends when drafting the actual text, because the writer will be sure of the approach and will be working to a plan.

DEVELOP A FIRST DRAFT

Developing documents is a process that involves several steps rather than a single act. Many writers have unreasonable expectations, assuming that in one step they can move from draft to final on a document. That may be possible for simple or standardized letters, especially if the writer has written a similar document several times, but in most complex organizations, writers are confronted with new challenges, not well-rehearsed behaviors. Detailed, complex, or technical letters require a number of steps.

Some writers develop writer's block, an inability to face a blank page. These writers might begin again and again, trying to craft the first sentence. Or they simply may procrastinate, finding other work to do and putting off writing until they are faced with an imminent deadline.

If the writer follows the process recommended thus far (thinking about purpose and audience, planning through outlining), he or she has already started writing and should be on the way to a strong draft. Writing is never easy, but planning makes it easier and more likely to be effective. Making progress in planning a document feels good, and the momentum keeps the writer progressing.

There are other ways to get a good start on a draft document. Consider these techniques:

- Talk through the document with a colleague.
- Make a list of everything the document should accomplish.
- Make a list of key words to be used in the document.
- Try drafting by writing as quickly as possible; then go back and make sense of what is on paper.

- Set aside time without interruption. Turn on the answering machine, ignore the e-mail, and close the door. Writing requires concentration.
- Work first on the most familiar or easiest parts. Begin writing at the middle, end, or beginning of the document, whatever is easiest and gets the words flowing.
- With long documents, work for a given amount of time, perhaps an hour, and then put it away until the next day, and then work again for an hour. Make steady progress.
- Use the word processor as a tool to help generate ideas, see connections, and keep track of thoughts. If the writer is working in one section and has a good idea for another section, stop and make a note. Use "stickies," index cards, notepaper, or leave placeholders to record information to be inserted later in sections or paragraphs.
- End a drafting session with a few notes about where to begin the next drafting session. Leave a place to begin on the next round.

Drafting is primarily about flow—getting flow, keeping flow going, managing flow. Many people notice that once they get the flow going, writing becomes quite satisfying and they even resent interruptions. Attend to personal work patterns and recognize how to attain and maintain flow while drafting complex documents.

Bring Others into the Process

Documents like letters and proposals should be shared with a colleague for peer review. Getting a review improves the writing and helps to identify problems that may not be obvious to the writer. Peer reviewers should offer constructive and objective criticism of the work. They can read in the role of the audience. Once you have a draft in place, even if it is quite rough, be prepared to share it with others in your office.

Writers benefit when they let others look at their drafts, especially at an early stage. Doing this involves a certain level of trust and openness, especially if the writer is asking a subordinate to look at an early draft. Reviewers should be asked to do more than say "Put a semicolon here" or "Why don't you say *donor* instead of *patron?*" They should play the role of the intended reader and tell the writer how they *feel* and *react* as they read the writing:

- Do they understand the writer's purpose?
- Do they understand the writer's goals?
- Do they feel respected and understood as the audience of the document?
- Do they feel persuaded that what the writer is asking for is reasonable, important, and good?
- Do they feel the document has the right information?
- Do they feel the document has the best strategy to accomplish its goals?

Many people are protective of their drafts and do not want other people to see work until it is finished. This is a mistake. The nonprofit organization needs to create a writing culture inside the organization, a culture that recognizes the value of teamwork and collaborative writing. A good way to do this is for the natural leaders in the organization to take the lead, share documents with others, and create an environment where people expect to help each other in significant ways.

MANAGE DOCUMENTS TO MEET DEADLINES

Planned giving documents must be planned, organized, developed, and managed to meet deadlines. Proper planning can make deadlines a helpful rather than a stressful experience.

Timing

When planning a document, allow time for the various stages of planning, drafting, reviewing, revising, and preparing the final document to be published. Getting *something* on paper early in the process provides material to work with and helps create a sense of progress. Building early drafts and early reviews into your timetable ensures that documents have time to develop. Rushed work in desperate response to deadlines is not going to produce strong writing.

Project Planning

Many time management and project management tools are on the market, and seminars are offered regularly on these topics. Adopt what is out there or invent an approach and tools. Most people benefit from a structured approach, supported by some kind of written plan, with activities, dates, staffing, and deliverables clearly marked. Treat writing as a work activity and map it out, working from the due date back through all the associated activities. This kind of backward planning, or planning with the end in mind, is essential for major initiatives, as when preparing marketing materials such as a "Guide to Charitable Giving." When finishing a big project, get the team together, look over the original plan, and figure out whether the project was well planned, where more time was needed, and how to manage things better on the next project.

File Organization

Complicated documents take time and care to write. A bank of planned giving letters and other documents can help writers meet deadlines. Properly label documents on computer or disk, with well-organized directories and files, to reduce the time spent searching for documents. Creating a document name—which includes the file name, date, and directory location or path for each document—is a great way to store and manage documents. Sometimes people spend more time looking for a document than writing it.

As the writer develops organized files, select some documents as models for new writers. While each writing situation is to some extent unique and must be responsive to particular details, many writers benefit from seeing good models. Also, the organization benefits from developing shared standards when it attempts to identify the best, most successful documents in its possession.

As nonprofit organizations mature, so do their document strategies. Many organizations develop a database of high-quality graphics and boilerplate text (text that can be reused in different documents). This is good practice, as long as the writer remembers to think about the *current* purpose and audience and strategically adapt the boilerplate. Fully mature organizations take advantage of technology by creating shared drives, where the organization's files are carefully stored and available to everyone in the group, so people do not waste time trying to find files on other people's machines or in file cabinets.

Design an Effective Document

Document production technologies have raised expectations for professional writing, and nonprofit staff must work hard to develop printed materials that are professional looking, usable, and effective. Marketing materials like brochures, newsletters, and guides need careful design to organize their content and to make them attractive to the reader. Carefully select the paper stock, font, color, graphics, number of columns, and width of columns; all affect the look and the impact of the document.

Try to write documents that are visually effective. Ask whether your readers can immediately sense the purpose of the document. If a specific request is being made, is that request in a prominent position, so the donor knows the point of the document? Is there adequate white space between blocks of print, with short paragraphs and nice wide margins? Has the writer chosen print in at least 12 point, since many readers have fading eyesight? Since many traditional planned giving donors are growing older, consider increasing the writing to 13 or 14 point.

For example, note the impact of different point type:

10 Point: Writing well is an important skill in Planned Giving.

12 Point: Writing well is an important skill in Planned Giving.

14 Point: Writing well is an important skill in Planned Giving.

16 Point: Writing well is an important skill in Planned Giving.

Most adults need 12-point print for body paragraphs.

Avoid overusing italics, especially for body paragraphs. It may suggest a more personal, handwritten approach to you, but in fact it is harder to read. Improve readability by adding a little extra space between lines of print and by not making the lines too long (30 to 40 characters per line is good). Space breaks between paragraphs and sections is also a good idea. If people must fill in forms, give them plenty of room to write and good directions.

Are documents legible, with good contrast of print on paper? Try to keep the documents looking clean; do not obscure your message with lots of clip art or by playing around with fonts and styles. Some organizations overdesign their materials, using too much color. Others print text over graphics or watermarks, making the materials difficult to read. Select a look and a design that match the professional character of the organization.

Documents must be appealing and attractive but not necessarily expensive. Select a design that is pleasing to the eye. Select paper that is an appropriate weight and color for the document. A very pleasing document can be created with a light-colored paper stock (buff or bone) together with a deep blue ink and perhaps one spot color to highlight the information and design.

Glitz increases the cost. Three-color (or more) pieces look great, but they must be produced at tremendous cost. Higher costs mean that fewer can be printed and mailed, thus reducing your ability to reach those who need to hear the nonprofit's message. Most donors are conscious of costs and value substance over form.

Consider developing a style guide for all your publications. You want to form an identity with your readers, so they know and trust you. This can be accomplished in part by producing distinctive documents that your audiences recognize as symbols of your organization.

TAKE ADVANTAGE OF DESKTOP PUBLISHING

Desktop publishing has brought the world of printed communications to a new level. Offices can now produce printed materials that are as good as, or better than, what can be bought. Instead of generically produced materials, the product can reflect the nonprofit organization's personality. To do the job well, quality computer hardware, software, and an experienced designer are needed. There are a number of appropriate hardware and software packages to choose from. Shop to find the best package to accommodate marketing needs and objectives. The largest expense will come in the first year; after that a budget can be established to purchase updates and enhancements. A first-year budget of $4,000 to $5,000 should be adequate to establish the program, and $500 to $1,000 each year thereafter should sustain the effort.

Operator

Desktop publishing software packages are complex, and it is too much to assume that a skilled word processor can excel at desktop publishing. An operator should be sent to a training course, commonly offered at colleges and universities, in the specific software selected. The investment in time and money is well worth it. If possible, the operator should be a part of the planned giving team and be involved in the early stages. It helps if a positive relationship develops between the writer and the operator since the production of these documents requires teamwork, feedback, and collaboration.

If possible, bring in a graphic designer or document designer to help create brochures, posters, templates, letterhead, business cards, and perhaps a logo for the group. All these establish an identity for the organization. Talk to the people at a local college—those in technical and professional communication or graphic design. Sponsor a student project or internship and line up some talented students to help with design in the organization.

Evaluation

Consider assembling a focus group to assess the publications and their usefulness. For example, assemble on a table the documents and publications used in the past year in the nonprofit organization. Get the team together. Bring in a couple of supportive donors or clients. Bring in the design person or someone from the university design or writing program. Look at the documents from a distance. Are they attractive? Do they make you want to read them? Do they look professional? Do they look like they come from the same organization, one with a confident and established identity? Self-evaluations and focus groups provide valuable feedback on the effectiveness of organizational publications.

USE LANGUAGE CORRECTLY AND EFFECTIVELY

A planned giving officer spends time learning the content of planned giving: the ins and outs of the law, the ways that organizations are structured, the various forms of giving and their benefits and limitations. It is also important that the officer be in absolute control of grammar and cultivate a strong professional style. Here we offer principles for effective control of language to improve documents. Study these principles to sharpen the nonprofit's planned giving documents. Read and reread Strunk and White's wonderful text, *The Elements of Style*. A strong professional style is something to work toward.

Use Informal and Personal Words.   Some words bring a personal and conversational tone to correspondence. Referring to the nonprofit as *we* and to the prospective donor as *you* will create a sense of immediacy, something close to a conversation. The goal is to sound like a real person, a lively and interesting person, someone who is animated and optimistic about the organization's prospects. Do not go too far—do not offend by being too personal or pushy or by straining too hard to be funny.

Develop a light touch, a style that says the writer is not stuffy or pretentious, just someone trying to do a good job and enjoying it.

Example: The decision has been made by the organization to solicit donations for an endowed fund with the goal of supporting students of color in their pursuit of higher education.

Suggestion: We've decided to raise an endowment to support our talented minority students.

Write Using Active Verbs.   Active verbs create active messages, particularly when the one doing the action is the subject and the action is captured by an active verb. Verbs provide the center of the sentence and can make writing sharp, clear, and lively. Sentences with passive or "to be" verbs (*is, are, was, were, be, being, been*) slow writing down and take away energy. Active verbs convey more than the action—they establish a sense of tone and the writer's attitude.

The following passive examples are rewritten to active suggestions:

Example: It would be much appreciated if your reply were received by our office . . .

Suggestion: Please tell us what you think!

Example: It has been brought to the attention of the committee that gifts of real estate . . .

Suggestion: The committee understands that gifts of real estate . . .

Basic sentence structure calls for a subject followed by an active verb. Active verbs carry the action and are the most important words in the sentence. Compare these examples, where the writer finds the active verb and moves it closer to the subject:

Example: Through planned giving, the donor is provided with a sense of satisfaction.

Suggestion: Planned gifts satisfy the donor's wish to provide ongoing support.

Example: One option is provided by appreciated securities, which include such investment vehicles as stocks, bonds, and mutual funds . . .

Suggestion: Appreciated securities (stocks, bonds, and mutual funds) provide an option to . . .

Do Not Be Verbose.   Large words are not necessarily better than small words. Most of us pick up the language of our workplace, and, unfortunately, much of what is said or written is verbose or grandiose. This style frustrates readers and creates letters that do not communicate well. Large words fill space but seldom help readers understand the point of the letter. Clean up these sentences, excise words that perform no function, say what is meant, and do not be driven by high-sounding phrases. Many adjectives and adverbs take up space and accomplish little.

Avoid Jargon.   Jargon is language that is used by individuals employed by a particular business or industry. The language of planned giving is full of legal and tax jargon: *appreciated securities, charitable income tax deductions, discount rates, tangible personal property, generation-skipping transfer tax,* and *charitable remainder trust.* Although these words must and should be used in writing, they must not be used exclusively when dealing with individual donors and prospects. When they are used, explanatory language must translate the concept to something readers understand. If a technical concept must be used, offer readers a scenario or a small example that allows them to understand the concept in terms of familiar situations and actions. Each reader has a different level of understanding, and it is important to personalize the message to meet the needs of a particular reader.

Do Not Overqualify.   Qualifiers, routinely included in business and professional communications, detract from the message. Qualifiers include words or expressions like *sort of, quite, very, perhaps,* or *almost.* These words affect the clarity of the message and effectiveness.

Example: The rate is quite high . . .

Suggestion: The rate is 8% . . .

Eliminate Windy Word Clusters.   Windy word clusters includes phrases such as these: *in order to, in the event that, needless to say, in regard to, as a consequence of,* and *as a matter of fact.* Like qualifiers, these phrases add nothing to the writing and only serve to cloud the message, which, for planned giving purposes, may already be confusing.

Example: In order to transfer the stock . . .

Suggestion: To transfer stock . . .

Be Careful with "Th" Words: A number of words that begin with "th" can detract from the writing. Such words are used routinely to begin sentences, but they might appear anywhere. Words like *this, that, these,* and *those* create problems since they should refer to something that immediately preceded and that is in the reader's mind. Make sure the reference is clear. Or combine the sentences and avoid beginning new sentences with these words.

Example: Planned giving provides important financial benefits. This is attractive to many donors.

Suggestion: Planned giving provides important and attractive financial benefits to donors.

Be Economical and Direct. Words become sentences, sentences become paragraphs, and paragraphs become documents. Every English composition professor teaches the importance of one topic-one paragraph, a concept that is often forgotten. Some writers write in circles or in choppy short sentences. Linear writers move the information forward in a logical and orderly sequence, never missing a step or an opportunity to develop the message. Look for ways to be economical with words so the writing moves smoothly and quickly to fulfill the goals.

> **Example:** The charitable gift annuity pays a fixed rate and provides a tax deduction. The deduction is $3,960. This means the actual gain for someone in the 31% tax bracket is 9%.
>
> **Suggestion:** The charitable gift annuity pays a fixed rate of 7% and provides a charitable income tax deduction of $3,960, representing an after-tax gain of 9% (for someone in the 31% tax bracket).

Use Parallel Structure. Parallel structure means using similar grammatical constructions to express similar ideas. Parallel structures give writing balance and elegance.

> **Example:** Many donors make gifts directly to the planned giving office, while the preference of others is to work through their bank and some like to use their broker.
>
> **Suggestion:** While many donors make gifts directly to the planned giving office, others work through their bankers or brokers.

Notice how *bankers* and *brokers* become part of an economical, parallel, compound phrase.

When used in series, words ending in "ing," "ed," and "en" should have consistent endings.

> **Example:** The art will be inventoried, and after cataloging, there will be a display . . .
>
> **Suggestion:** The art will be inventoried, cataloged, and displayed . . .

Conclusion

This chapter has offered productive ways to prepare documents to help writers become better communicators for planned giving. Developing documents will not suddenly become easy; it is likely to remain hard work, although one hopes it is satisfying. Get others involved and make it a team effort. Always remember how much documents are related to success, since they are a primary means of communicating with those who are ready to help perform the good work of the nonprofit organization.

Documents include a variety of key elements. Ignoring or omitting one can destroy the impact of a document. The recipe to produce quality documents includes one-fourth of each of the following ingredients:

- *Strategy.* Strategy is the planning, preparation, and collaboration in document production.
- *Content.* Content is the substance of the message.
- *Design.* Design is the proper look, layout, and format of the document.
- *Language.* Language includes the use of proper and effective sentence structure, strong word choice, and correct punctuation.

Above all, remember that planned giving letters, marketing materials, and exhibits help to reinforce the image and sustain the relationship of the nonprofit organization with donors. These documents, properly structured with effective messages, attract planned giving donors and prospects. Documents are important tools in the business of planned giving. Use them wisely and the nonprofit will be rewarded.

Important Reminder

At the time this book went into production, the Internal Revenue Service was considering issuing revised charitable remainder trust model forms. Once issued, readers should obtain copies of these documents and ask the nonprofit organization's general counsel or other outside legal counsel to evaluate the impact of these changes on forms currently being used and also on forms contained within this text. Please remember that all CD-ROM documents need to be modified to reflect the current tax law and the ever-changing discount rate.

## CHAPTER 1

Marketing Materials

INTRODUCTION

Running a planned giving program is similar to starting a business. Successful businesses are clear about the products they offer, understand the audience they are trying to reach, and use marketing strategies to attract the targeted audience. Nonprofit organizations also must market. Marketing, in this case, means educating donors, prospects, faculty, staff volunteers, and all other nonprofit constituents about the nonprofit's services and needs. Marketing is a comprehensive, integrated campaign designed to raise awareness and stimulate interest. Marketing materials create a heightened level of visibility and project a positive image about the planned giving program and the nonprofit organization. In addition, marketing educates prospects about planned giving vehicles and articulates the mission of the nonprofit organization. This chapter discusses the marketing materials needed to market and promote a planned giving program to donors, prospects, and other constituents.

DOCUMENTS

This chapter and the documents included in Section 1 of the CD-ROM focus exclusively on Marketing. The CD-ROM contains 75 documents that perform the functions described in this chapter. In addition the following documents are specifically referenced and included in this chapter:

Document 2	Planned Giving Mini-Guide
Document 55A	Life Income Gifts
Document 44	Establishing a Named Scholarship
Document 9	Gift of Appreciated Securities
Document 34	Gifts of Real Estate
Document 53	Charitable Gift Annuities and Pooled Income Funds
Document 55B	Response Form to Newsletter
Document 69	Establishing an Endowed Fund

GUIDE TO CHARITABLE GIFT PLANNING

A guide to charitable gift planning or a "Ways to Give" brochure outlines the many ways that a donor can make a gift to a nonprofit using a wide variety of assets (see Exhibit 1-1). This brochure is probably the most important marketing document in planned giving because it provides so much detail about planned giving options. It may be simple or fancy. The important thing is to have a brochure that outlines the different ways to give, shows various giving levels and gift minimums, and provides information on tax, financial planning, and estate planning. A typical table of contents includes:

- *Description of the nonprofit organization.* This section reinforces the prominent and unique features of the organization and emphasizes the distinct characteristics that separate this nonprofit from other nonprofits. Highlights can be shown in bulleted form. A nonprofit organization should include a mission statement, a brief history, and a description of services and programs it offers to constituents.

- *About the development office.* This part describes the charitable giving and planned giving services and programs available to prospects and donors. The writing should consider the needs of the reader and should be designed to open the door to inquiries and encourage communication between the organization and its constituents.

- *Menu of assets.* This section tells donors the broadest range of asset options that can be used to make gifts. These options include cash, securities, retirement plans, real estate, and tangible personal property, collections, and other types of noncash assets. The menu encourages donors to consider a broad array of assets. Charities always should promote gifts of assets that are related to their charitable purposes. For example, museums should promote gifts of art collections; operas and symphonies could promote collections of valuable music scores or antique musical instruments.

- *Planned giving options.* This section should include a complete discussion of each of the planned giving vehicles that the nonprofit offers. It should not be overly technical but should pique a donor's interest rather than be an authoritative, technically focused presentation. Include charitable gift annuities, deferred gift annuities, the pooled income fund, charitable remainder trusts, life insurance, and bequests. Use charts or tables to illustrate and organize financial benefits.

- *Endowed funding levels and naming opportunities.* This section should provide a summary of the organization's funding levels and include information about naming opportunities for establishing chairs, endowed funds, professorships, institutes, and scholarships. Minimum giving levels help to raise donors' sights for making larger gifts. Naming opportunities promote gifts at significant levels, encouraging donors to permanently link their names with the charity's.

- *Leadership and recognition societies.* These societies help donors to feel a part of a larger group. Some donors are motivated to increase their giving to reach certain giving club levels. Include the name of the planned giving society and list its benefits to members, including special mailings, annual meetings or events, and other membership benefits. Many charities recognize a donor's cumulative giving record for gift levels of $10,000, $25,000, $50,000, $100,000, $250,000, $500,000, $1,000,000, and up. Many donors make gifts to "graduate" to the next level.

- *Staff.* Decide whether to include individual staff members' names, titles, telephone numbers, and e-mail addresses to help facilitate contact between staff and donors. Unfortunately, when individual employees leave, this information becomes out of date. Nonprofit organizations may simply include the titles of employees and a description of their duties.

Once the brochure is printed, send it to donors who request information about making a gift to the organization and bring a copy when making personal visits. Other development officers also can use it when meeting with donors to talk about making a gift. Print additional copies to meet future needs. Keep in mind that tax laws constantly change so do not substantially overprint gift brochures.

EXHIBIT 1-1.   PLANNED GIVING MINI-GUIDE DOCUMENT

This document is an abbreviated version of the longer "Guide to Charitable Gift Planning." It contains the basic gift options and addresses ways to make gifts using a variety of assets. The document contains information on life income gifts, charitable remainder trusts, estate planning, and endowed funds.

DOCUMENT 2

PLANNED GIVING MINI-GUIDE

Tax Planning and Charitable Giving at ‹ORGANIZATION›

The Office of Development presents donors with financial options that benefit both the donors and ‹ORGANIZATION›. Most of our financial vehicles, such as gift annuities, deferred gift annuities, the pooled income fund, and trusts, provide the donor with income for life. These vehicles pay a rate of return that often exceeds money market and CD rates. In addition, some of these vehicles avoid capital gains taxes and reduce estate taxes. We also work with donors who make gifts through their estates while preserving assets for their current needs. Let us help you while you help ‹ORGANIZATION› by making a gift to ‹ORGANIZATION›.

EXHIBIT 1-1.   PLANNED GIVING MINI-GUIDE DOCUMENT *(Continued)*

Gift by Check

A gift by check may be made outright or pledged over a period of up to five years. If you itemize your tax deductions, your gift is fully deductible up to 50% of your adjusted gross income. Any excess can be carried forward for up to five additional years.

Appreciated Securities

Your outright gift of long-term, appreciated securities (stocks, mutual funds, and bonds) is exempt from capital gains taxes and, in most cases, enables you to obtain a charitable income tax deduction equal to the market value of the securities at the time of transfer for up to 30% of your adjusted gross income. Any excess can be carried over for up to five additional years.

Life Income Gifts

A donor can make a gift to ‹ORGANIZATION› and receive direct financial benefits. The benefits include an income for life for the donor and/or the donor's spouse and a charitable income tax deduction. The charitable gift annuity, pooled income fund, and deferred gift annuity require a minimum gift of ‹ $ ›, which may be designated to benefit any department or program at ‹ORGANIZATION›.

Charitable Gift Annuity

A gift annuity is a contract between the donor and ‹ORGANIZATION› that provides advantages to both. The donor makes a gift and receives a guaranteed payment for life and a charitable income tax deduction. The payout rate on a gift annuity is based on the age of the donor at the time the gift is made. Charitable gift annuities may be funded with cash, securities, or property. Payouts may be made annually, semiannually, quarterly, or monthly.

BENEFITS FROM A $5,000 CHARITABLE GIFT ANNUITY*

Age	Payout Rate	Annual Income	Tax Deduction
65	‹ % ›	‹ $ ›	‹ $ ›
70	‹ % ›	‹ $ ›	‹ $ ›
75	‹ % ›	‹ $ ›	‹ $ ›
80	‹ % ›	‹ $ ›	‹ $ ›

*Figures based on current discount rate of ‹ % ›.

The Pooled Income Fund

The pooled income fund is similar to a mutual fund. Your gift is pooled with other donors' gifts and assigned a proportionate interest in the fund. The rate is variable and currently pays ‹ % › to each participant. You may name a second beneficiary to receive a life income from your gift after your death. Ultimately, the gift will pass to ‹ORGANIZATION› to be used in accordance with your wishes.

EXHIBIT 1-1.   PLANNED GIVING MINI-GUIDE DOCUMENT *(Continued)*

BENEFITS FROM A $5,000 GIFT TO THE POOLED INCOME FUND*

Age	Payout Rate	Annual Income	Tax Deduction
50	‹ % ›	‹ $ ›	‹ $ ›
55	‹ % ›	‹ $ ›	‹ $ ›
60	‹ % ›	‹ $ ›	‹ $ ›
65	‹ % ›	‹ $ ›	‹ $ ›
70	‹ % ›	‹ $ ›	‹ $ ›

*Figures based on current discount rate of ‹ % ›.

Deferred Gift Annuity

A deferred gift annuity is similar to a charitable gift annuity, except that the payments are deferred to a future date. In addition, the donor obtains a substantial charitable income tax deduction in the year the gift is made. A deferred gift annuity is an excellent way for younger donors to make a gift and receive a charitable income tax deduction while providing income for the future.

BENEFITS FROM A $5,000 DEFERRED GIFT ANNUITY DEFERRED TO AGE 65*

Age	Payout Rate	Annual Income	Tax Deduction
30	‹ % ›	‹ $ ›	‹ $ ›
35	‹ % ›	‹ $ ›	‹ $ ›
40	‹ % ›	‹ $ ›	‹ $ ›
45	‹ % ›	‹ $ ›	‹ $ ›
50	‹ % ›	‹ $ ›	‹ $ ›

*Figures based on current discount rate of ‹ % ›.

Charitable Remainder Trust

A charitable remainder trust provides a lifetime income and a charitable income tax deduction. The donor selects the payout rate, usually between 5% and 7%. The higher the payout rate, the lower the charitable income tax deduction. This gives the donor, and perhaps the donor's spouse, an income every year for life.

Annuity Trust and Unitrust

- An annuity trust pays a fixed, guaranteed dollar amount regardless of the trust's investment performance.
- A unitrust pays the donor a predetermined percentage of the fair market value of the trust's assets as revalued annually.
- Capital gains taxes are avoided on transfers of appreciated assets.
- Estate taxes may be avoided or diminished.

EXHIBIT 1-1.   PLANNED GIVING MINI-GUIDE DOCUMENT *(Continued)*

BENEFITS FROM A $100,000 CHARITABLE REMAINDER TRUST FOR A DONOR AGE 70*

Payout Rate	Annual Income	Charitable Annuity Trust	Income Tax Unitrust
5%	‹ $ ›	‹ $ ›	‹ % ›
6%	‹ $ ›	‹ $ ›	‹ % ›
7%	‹ $ ›	‹ $ ›	‹ % ›
8%	‹ $ ›	‹ $ ›	‹ % ›

*Figures based on current discount rate of ‹ % ›.

Gifts of Real Estate

You can make a gift of commercial or residential real estate to ‹ORGANIZATION› and receive substantial financial benefits. If you wish to give the property outright, you qualify for a charitable income tax deduction based on the appraised value of the property. If you are contemplating leaving your home to ‹ORGANIZATION› through your will, you may want to consider giving it now but retaining the right to live in it for your lifetime. You will continue to pay taxes, insurance, and maintenance costs. However, by giving now, you receive a substantial charitable income tax deduction in the year the gift is made.

Gifts through Your Estate

For many donors, making a gift through their estates is the most realistic way to provide a substantial contribution to ‹ORGANIZATION›.

Summary of Benefits

A gift through your estate reduces or may eliminate federal estate taxes.

Most states provide estate or inheritance tax benefits for gifts through an estate to non-profit organizations.

Specific Bequest

‹ORGANIZATION› receives a specific dollar amount, a specific piece of property, or a stated percentage of the estate. This is one of the most popular forms of bequests.

Residuary Bequest

‹ORGANIZATION› receives all or a stated percentage of an estate after distribution of specific bequests and payment of debts, taxes, and expenses.

Contingent Bequest

‹ORGANIZATION› receives part or all of the estate under certain specified circumstances.

Trust Established under a Will

A trust may be established that provides for both ‹ORGANIZATION› and other beneficiaries.

EXHIBIT 1-1.   PLANNED GIVING MINI-GUIDE DOCUMENT *(Continued)*

Scholarship Funds

Endowed scholarship funds provide financial assistance to worthy and needy students at ‹ORGANIZATION›. Scholarship funds can be tailored to meet your specific goals.

Endowed Scholarships

The minimum level at ‹ORGANIZATION› is ‹ $ › to establish a named endowed scholarship fund. You may fund it now with cash, or fund it partially or completely through a planned gift and/or through a bequest from your estate.

Current-Use Scholarships

Current-use scholarship funds are awarded the year the gift is made. These funds do not grow but provide immediate financial assistance to ‹ORGANIZATION› students. You can create a named current-use scholarship for as little as ‹ $ ›.

Your Own Endowment Fund

Creating an endowed fund provides permanent support to ‹ORGANIZATION› for teaching, learning, and research each year in perpetuity. The endowed funds of many friends of ‹ORGANIZATION› have helped fund projects, scholarships, professorships, lecture series, athletic programs, operation of facilities, and much more.

There may be no finer way to honor the memory of a loved one than to establish a scholarship or an endowed professorship in his or her name. A named endowed fund becomes a lasting symbol of the bond between ‹ORGANIZATION› and those who are permanently honored.

Endowed Naming Opportunities

Distinguished ‹ORGANIZATION› Chair	‹ $ ›
‹ORGANIZATION› Chair	‹ $ ›
Professorship	‹ $ ›
Lectureship	‹ $ ›
Scholar-in-Residence	‹ $ ›
Full Tuition Scholarship	
Room and Board	‹ $ ›
Fellowship	‹ $ ›
Full Tuition Scholarship	‹ $ ›
Endowed Fund	‹ $ ›

Policies vary on guidelines for naming opportunities, some of which require approval.

Office of Development

Our staff is available to assist you in achieving your tax, estate planning, and charitable giving objectives. We are pleased to provide personal financial projections to you and your

---

EXHIBIT 1-1.   PLANNED GIVING MINI-GUIDE DOCUMENT *(Continued)*

---

financial advisors. For further information, please complete and return the response form below or call ‹TELEPHONE›.

‹ORGANIZATION›
Office of Development

Please send me more information about:

☐ Establishing a named fund   ☐ Making gifts of real estate

☐ Making a gift of appreciated securities   ☐ Making a gift through life insurance

☐ Receiving income from my gift   ☐ Providing for ‹ORGANIZATION› in my will

Name: _____

Address: _____

City: _____

State: _____ Zip: _____

Phone: _____

Send to: ‹NAME›, ‹TITLE›
            ‹ADDRESS›
            ‹CITY, STATE ZIP›
            ‹TELEPHONE›

NEWSLETTERS

A planned giving or development newsletter is a powerful tool for marketing a planned giving program. Create a newsletter on a specific topic and devote the entire issue to planned giving options or a specific gift vehicle, such as gifts of real estate or charitable remainder trusts. Newsletters enable charities to focus on a planned gift option or gifts of partial assets. Consider including planned giving articles, ads, and testimonials in a development newsletter that is distributed organization-wide to donors and prospects. Newsletters also can target specific audiences. Segment planned giving prospects into approximate age brackets, and write a newsletter about deferred gift annuities and send it to donors or prospects who are in the 30- to 50-year range, who would be most interested in learning about them. Similarly, consider producing a newsletter that features pooled income fund gifts or charitable gift annuities and send it to donors and prospects in appropriate age groups. In this way, you target the message to donors who would benefit most.

Also consider segmenting a newsletter by geographical areas to match with asset options. For example, a newsletter that focuses on gifts of land may be sent to prospects in rural areas where individuals may have more extensive real estate holdings (see Exhibit 1-2). A newsletter that features stock options can be directed to prospects in metropolitan areas. Remember to send the newsletter to outside advisors to enhance professional outreach.

EXHIBIT 1-2. LIFE INCOME GIFTS DOCUMENT

This newsletter focuses on life income gifts including charitable gift annuities, deferred gift annuities, and pooled income fund gifts. It explains the need for private support and suggests gift options that donors may use to provide financial support. You can modify the document to reflect the specific gift options offered by the nonprofit.

DOCUMENT 55A

LIFE INCOME GIFTS

Vol. ‹VOLUME NUMBER›   ‹PUBLICATION DATE›

‹ORGANIZATION›
Newsletter
‹ORGANIZATION›: Life Income Gifts

For donors and friends who wish to benefit ‹ORGANIZATION› and obtain a life income, three of our most popular planned giving vehicles are the charitable gift annuity, the pooled income fund, and the deferred gift annuity. These options allow donors to make a gift to benefit any department or program at ‹ORGANIZATION›; receive an income for life and perhaps for a spouse's lifetime; and obtain a charitable income tax deduction at the time the gift is made. The pooled income fund has an additional advantage in that gifts of appreciated securities can be made to the fund and the donor will completely avoid capital gains taxes. These three vehicles require a minimum of ‹ $ ›.

Charitable Gift Annuity

A charitable gift annuity is a contract between the donor and ‹ORGANIZATION›. For example, an 80-year-old donor who makes a ‹ $ › gift to a particular fund receives a ‹ % › rate of return, which amounts to ‹ $ › a year for the rest of the donor's life. In the year the gift is made, the donor receives a charitable income tax deduction of ‹ $ ›. The high rate of return and large charitable income tax deduction are most attractive to older donors.

EXHIBIT 1-2.   LIFE INCOME GIFTS DOCUMENT *(Continued)*

The Pooled Income Fund

The ‹ORGANIZATION› Pooled Income Fund is similar to a mutual fund. For example, assume a 65-year-old donor makes a ‹ $ › gift to the fund and receives a variable annual income (currently ‹ % ›), which amounts to ‹ $ › a year. In this case, the charitable income tax deduction is ‹ $ ›. If the gift is funded with appreciated securities, the donor pays no capital gains taxes.

The Deferred Gift Annuity

A deferred gift annuity is an excellent gift option that benefits younger donors, who receive an outstanding rate at a later age, often age 65. For example, a 40-year-old donor who makes a ‹ $ › gift to a particular scholarship fund of his or her choice receives a ‹ % › rate of return, or ‹ $ › a year, beginning at age 65. In addition, the donor obtains a charitable income tax deduction of ‹ $ › in the year the gift is made.

These gift options can be used to fund scholarships created by the donor or to benefit a particular department or program, such as the ‹PROGRAM/DEPARTMENT›. What a wonderful way to give to ‹ORGANIZATION› and receive excellent benefits!

The chart below illustrates the benefits a donor would realize from a gift of ‹ $ ›. Simply find your age under each gift option and read across for the rate, annual income, and charitable income tax deduction.

FOR A GIFT OF $10,000*

	Age	Rate	Income/Yr.	Tax Ded.
Charitable Gift Annuity	70	‹ % ›	‹ $ ›	‹ $ ›
	75	‹ % ›	‹ $ ›	‹ $ ›
	80	‹ % ›	‹ $ ›	‹ $ ›
Pooled Income Fund	55	‹ % ›	‹ $ ›	‹ $ ›
	60	‹ % ›	‹ $ ›	‹ $ ›
	65	‹ % ›	‹ $ ›	‹ $ ›
Deferred Gift Annuity	40	‹ % ›	‹ $ ›	‹ $ ›
	45	‹ % ›	‹ $ ›	‹ $ ›
	50	‹ % ›	‹ $ ›	‹ $ ›

*The figures presented are based on the current discount rate of ‹ % ›.

To Our Readers

Revenue at ‹ORGANIZATION› provides ‹ % › percent of our total operating costs, so to meet our annual budget we need the financial support of donors, friends, and corporations and foundations. During fiscal ‹YEAR› more than ‹NUMBER› donors, friends, and corporations and foundations helped support programs at ‹ORGANIZATION›.

The purpose of offering gift opportunities and financial options is to mutually benefit both donors and ‹ORGANIZATION›. Most of our financial vehicles, such as gift annuities, deferred

---

EXHIBIT 1-2.   LIFE INCOME GIFTS DOCUMENT *(Continued)*

---

gift annuities, the pooled income fund, and charitable remainder trusts, provide the donor with income. These vehicles pay a rate that often exceeds money market and CD rates. In addition, some of these options avoid capital gains taxes and increase a donor's current dividends.

<ORGANIZATION> also works with donors who wish to make a bequest, which is a clause in a will that enables them to make gifts through their estates while preserving assets for their current needs. Through bequests, donors may leave a specific dollar amount or a percentage of their estate to <ORGANIZATION>. Outright gifts and pledges are also welcome. Please contact us for further information and let us show you how we can help you while you help <ORGANIZATION>.

PLANNED GIVING COLUMNS IN DONOR PUBLICATIONS

A planned giving column placed in an organization's newspaper, magazine, or newsletter affords another opportunity to communicate with planned giving donors and prospects. Emphasize just one single planned giving vehicle or gift option per issue. Doing this creates a wonderful opportunity to develop a library of informative, in-depth columns over time. These columns can be reprinted and sent as supplementary information to donors. They also can serve as the basis of a feature article in a newsletter as well as training materials for staff. You may wish to include a picture of the staff so that donors become more familiar with the planned giving personnel. Include a response box with each column to facilitate requests for information. A sample planned giving column appears in Exhibit 1-3.

EXHIBIT 1-3.   LIFE INCOME GIFTS: NAMED SCHOLARSHIPS

A column can be placed in a variety of a nonprofit organization's printed materials. This column focuses on ways donors can establish endowed scholarship funds and life income gifts and explains the way the gift option works. It is designed to encourage readers to ask for additional information.

DOCUMENT 44

ESTABLISHING A NAMED SCHOLARSHIP

Endowed Scholarships

Endowed scholarship funds provide much-needed financial assistance to worthy and needy students at <ORGANIZATION>.

EXHIBIT 1-3.   LIFE INCOME GIFTS: NAMED SCHOLARSHIPS *(Continued)*

Scholarship funds can be tailored to meet your specific goals. First, you must decide whom you're trying to benefit. You may choose to provide assistance to a student studying a specific major or in a particular program at ‹ORGANIZATION›. You may decide whether the recipient should be a graduate or an undergraduate, and whether the candidate must be financially needy and academically worthy to receive the award.

You must also decide how to fund the scholarship. The minimum level at ‹ORGANIZATION› is ‹ $ › to establish a named endowed scholarship fund. You may fund it now with cash, or fund it partially or completely through a planned gift or through a bequest from your estate. If you establish the fund now, you have the opportunity to be recognized for your participation and will be able to meet the recipient.

Your named fund can grow with the help of friends and family. You can make additional gifts at any time. Often relatives and friends make gifts in lieu of birthday or holiday presents.

Current-Use Scholarships

An alternative to an endowed scholarship is a current-use fund. Current-use scholarship funds are spent in the year the gift is made and are for unrestricted scholarship purposes. These funds do not grow but provide financial assistance to ‹ORGANIZATION› students. You can create a named current-use scholarship for as little as ‹ $ ›. Why not enable a deserving student to benefit from the educational opportunities at ‹ORGANIZATION›?

For information about establishing a scholarship fund, please contact ‹ORGANIZATION›, ‹NAME›, ‹TITLE›, ‹ADDRESS›, ‹CITY, STATE ZIP› or call ‹TELEPHONE›.

CONVENTIONAL ADVERTISEMENTS

Use planned giving advertisements that can be placed in newsletters, organization newspapers, or magazines to attract new business to the planned giving program (see Exhibit 1-4). Consider drafting straightforward, uncomplicated informational ads with bullets to illustrate various gift benefits. Use one ad per gift vehicle or concept, and do not hesitate to repeat publication of the same ad. The planned giving office can draft and prepare ads at little or no cost.

EXHIBIT 1-4.   GIFT OF APPRECIATED SECURITIES DOCUMENT

This ad promotes the benefits of a gift of appreciated securities. It takes little space but connects well with readers who are investors and can reinforce information previously included in brochures, newsletters, and columns.

EXHIBIT 1-4.   GIFT OF APPRECIATED SECURITIES DOCUMENT *(Continued)*

DOCUMENT 9

GIFT OF APPRECIATED SECURITIES

Do You Own Low-Yielding or Appreciated Securities?

The ‹ORGANIZATION› Pooled Income Fund can help you while you help ‹ORGANIZATION›. For a minimum gift of $5,000 you can:

- Increase your yield substantially (current rate is ‹ % ›)
- Avoid capital gains tax on gifts of appreciated securities
- Receive an income for life
- Receive an immediate charitable income tax deduction
- Become a member of a ‹ORGANIZATION› leadership club

The Office of Development will send you a personalized financial analysis that shows you how a contribution to the Pooled Income Fund can benefit both you and ‹ORGANIZATION›. Please contact ‹NAME›, ‹TITLE›, ‹ORGANIZATION›, ‹ADDRESS›, ‹CITY, STATE ZIP›; ‹TELEPHONE›.

BUCKSLIPS

Buckslips are a valuable, inexpensive form of communication that are included with a mailing. They usually are smaller than a full page, often the size of a dollar bill, hence the name buckslip. Like a reply device, a buckslip enables a prospect to ask for more information. Enclose buckslips with mailings such as an annual fund appeal or year-end tax letter. Use buckslips to encourage donors to request information about various life income gifts, establishing a named fund, and tax, financial, and estate planning information.

USE OF A BUCKSLIP

A bank, trust company, or utility company may allow a nonprofit organization to include information about the nonprofit's activities in the company's mailing. Distributing buckslips in company mailings may work best when the nonprofit is the biggest or best-known organization in that area. It also works well for small nonprofits in rural areas. It is not as likely to work in major cities where there are dozens of nonprofits, but nonprofits cannot be sure until they ask for permission. At one nonprofit organization, staff spoke with banks and utility companies about including buckslips with bank statements to customers (see Exhibit 1-5). The buckslips featured information about life income gifts and the ways in which these gifts can benefit donors and the nonprofit. A response form appeared on the reverse side of the card. Several banks included the buckslip in their bank statements, and over the years thousands of buckslips were distributed to bank customers who were potential prospects for the charity.

| EXHIBIT 1-5. | GIFTS OF REAL ESTATE DOCUMENT |

This buckslip promotes gifts of real estate. Buckslips provide more information and are stand-alone pieces that can be included in a variety of mailings. Place them in annual giving mailings or insert them into almost all of the nonprofit organization's publications. They generate interest and are inexpensive to produce.

DOCUMENT 34

GIFTS OF REAL ESTATE

‹ORGANIZATION›
Gifts of Real Estate

It pays to give to ‹ORGANIZATION›. There are many ways to make gifts of real estate, each of which affords many attractive benefits. Some of the options permit the donors to live in the property for their lifetimes while providing them an income and charitable income tax deduction. Depending on the option, benefits may enable donors to:

- Earn an income for life
- Produce a substantial charitable income tax deduction
- Reduce capital gains taxes
- Avoid probate costs
- Save estate taxes
- Avoid the burden of upkeep, property taxes, and insurance
- Receive a lump-sum payment, an income, and a charitable income tax deduction
- Use the gift to establish a scholarship or endowed fund

The Office of Development will be pleased to send you a personalized financial analysis that shows how a gift of real estate can benefit both you and ‹ORGANIZATION›. Please contact ‹NAME›, ‹TITLE›, ‹ADDRESS›, ‹CITY, STATE ZIP›; ‹TELEPHONE›.

TESTIMONIAL ADVERTISEMENTS

Testimonial ads are a wonderful way to illustrate the benefits of a planned gift. Such ads feature a donor or donors talking about the gift they made to the organization. These testimonials serve to educate other prospects about gift options, help them feel part of a larger group of donors, and spark a feeling of similarity between a donor considering making a gift and one who already has made a gift. Testimonials are easy to read and nontechnical (see Exhibit 1-6). They show "real-life" donors and tend to evoke an emotional response. It is important to include a picture of the donors with testimonial ads.

EXHIBIT 1-6.   TESTIMONIAL AD: CHARITABLE GIFT ANNUITIES

This testimonial ad features a gift by a donor who explains the benefits of a charitable gift annuity. The donor's picture typically is included with the ad. Testimonial ads are interesting to read. They illustrate how gifts can be made using a donor as a role model. Because of the size, they fit neatly into most publications. Alternatively, longer testimonial ads can profile key contributors containing detailed biographical sketches with complete gift descriptions.

DOCUMENT 53

CHARITABLE GIFT ANNUITIES AND POOLED INCOME FUNDS

Donor Profile

‹DONOR›

Establishes a Charitable Gift Annuity

"Because of my gift to ‹ORGANIZATION› through a Charitable Gift Annuity, I am able to have a substantial tax deduction and receive an income for the rest of my life! Most important, my Charitable Gift Annuity will benefit the ‹DEPARTMENT/PROGRAM›."

On ‹MONTH, DAY, YEAR›, ‹DONOR›, an ‹ORGANIZATION› alumnus, made a gift of ‹ $ › to establish a Charitable Gift Annuity. The annuity rate is ‹ % ›, payable monthly. ‹DONOR›'s charitable income tax deduction is ‹ $ ›, and annual income is ‹ $ ›, of which ‹ $ › is tax-free.

You can also take advantage of the benefits of a Charitable Gift Annuity. The minimum to establish a gift annuity is ‹ $ ›.

PLANNED GIVING PIECES IN LOCAL NEWSPAPERS

Test market a planned giving column or ad about life income gift options or gifts of real estate in a local newspaper or trade paper. Use a commercial newspaper to expand the donor population to include those not affiliated with the nonprofit but who could benefit from making a planned gift. Target appeals to the constituency reading the ad; for example, place planned giving ads for charitable gift annuities in newspapers that are read by an older population, located in the appropriate section of the newspaper. Remember to emphasize that these planned giving options are gift vehicles, not traditional investment options.

RESPONSE FORM

No communication or publication is complete without a reply device. The reply device, or response form, enables prospects to communicate with the planned giving office simply and easily. A perforated card, a card inserted into the spine of a booklet, or a tear-off device serves as an appropriate response form. The response form always should include the planned giving officer's address and telephone number and include a place for the prospect's name, address, telephone number, and age. The response form also should provide a place for the donor to indicate the anticipated asset to be used to make the gift, and the approximate size of the gift. Donors who complete this part of the response form provide valuable information about their gift capacity. See Exhibit 1-7 for a sample response form.

EXHIBIT 1-7.	RESPONSE FORM TO NEWSLETTER

This response form invites the reader to request additional information. A response form makes it easy for donors to request additional information and should accompany all documents. The response choices relate to information contained in the accompanying document.

DOCUMENT 55B

LIFE INCOME GIFTS

‹ORGANIZATION› Office of Development

Please send me more information about:

- ❑ Establishing a named fund
- ❑ Receiving income from my gift
- ❑ Providing for ‹ORGANIZATION› in my will
- ❑ Making a gift of appreciated securities
- ❑ Making a gift of real estate

EXHIBIT 1-7. RESPONSE FORM TO NEWSLETTER *(Continued)*

Name: _____

Address: _____

City: _____

State: _____ Zip: _____

Send to: ‹ORGANIZATON›
 ‹NAME›, ‹TITLE›
 ‹ADDRESS›
 ‹CITY, STATE ZIP›
 ‹TELEPHONE›

FACT SHEETS

Fact sheets provide basic and essential information about planned giving options. They are distributed to employees online through shared drives and to donors through the nonprofit organization's website. Most fact sheets are no more than one page. They provide the nuts and bolts about specific planned gift options including a brief description and other information about payout rates, income streams, and charitable income tax deductions. They generate leads from donors and provide information to staff members. They are not designed to be used without the assistance of a planned giving officer who must advise employees and donors about the specifics of the gift option and its appropriateness in a particular situation.

Shared drives are popular computer devices that enable certain nonprofit employees to access information provided by the development or planned giving office. Shared drives contain essential boilerplate information about the nonprofit organization, mission statements, and financial needs. Planned giving offices can include information about gift options, endowed funds, and the use of assets other than cash and can include sample bequest language. Staff members can download and print fact sheets for their own use or for a donor or department head. As with all general information, instruct users to consult with planned giving staff members to make certain that a particular gift option is appropriate for a donor.

Fact sheets also can be placed on the nonprofit organization's website to enable donors and prospects to learn about gift options that may be of interest to them. These fact sheets serve to educate constituents about planned giving concepts (see Exhibit 1-8). Donors and prospects often contact the planned giving office directly to confirm information or seek clarification.

EXHIBIT 1-8.	Establishing an Endowed Fund Document

This fact sheet illustrates the benefits to a donor in establishing an endowed fund. It can be placed both on the nonprofit organization's website and on shared drives.

DOCUMENT 69

ESTABLISHING AN ENDOWED FUND

Endowed funds provide financial assistance to benefit students, faculty, and much more. Donors may choose to support a variety of campus initiatives, such as faculty and staff enrichment programs, or to underwrite the costs of research, seminars, departmental program support, and capital projects. Private support makes the difference in the quality of programs that <ORGANIZATION> offers. Endowed funds promote excellence in education. Each endowed fund bears the name of the donor who established the fund.

Financing an Endowed Fund

A minimum of $10,000 is required to establish an endowed scholarship fund. Other types of funds have larger minimum requirements. You may specify in writing the purpose that your endowed fund is to serve and how the fund is to be administered.

Your named fund can grow with the help of family and friends. Additional gifts can be made at any time. Often relatives and friends make gifts in lieu of birthday or holiday presents. Your endowed fund may be funded through an outright gift, a planned gift, or a gift through one's estate.

How Endowed Funds Are Managed

The principal of the endowed fund is invested by <ORGANIZATION>, and a portion of the income earned is distributed in perpetuity. Annually, 5% of the market value of the fund is distributed in support of the fund's purpose. Excess earnings are added to principal to produce more income in future years. An annual fee of < % > is charged to cover the expenses of professional money management.

Selection Criteria

The donors must decide how the income earned on the endowed fund will be used. Donors may choose to benefit a student by providing scholarship assistance, or they may benefit faculty initiatives, academic programs, or a capital project. By creating an endowed fund, you make a lasting contribution to the future of <ORGANIZATION>.

EXHIBIT 1-8.   ESTABLISHING AN ENDOWED FUND DOCUMENT *(Continued)*

Endowed Funds in Honor or Memory of Loved Ones

Donors often establish endowments in memory or in honor of loved ones. Establishing an endowment is an excellent way of honoring the memory of a loved one. Endowed funds can also be established in honor of distinguished professors or other individuals who made a difference in your life.

Building Your Endowed Family Fund

Over the years, the Office of Planned Giving has helped families increase the size of their endowed family funds, and we are pleased to share with you some of our ideas. We welcome the opportunity to develop a plan to increase your family fund to provide additional benefits to the program of your choice at ‹ORGANIZATION›.

For more information, please feel free to contact ‹NAME›, Director of Planned Giving, at ‹ORGANIZATION› Office of Planned Giving, ‹ADDRESS, CITY, STATE ZIP, TELEPHONE›. We will be happy to assist you in making a gift to benefit ‹ORGANIZATION› and its students.

CONCLUSION

One of the most important components of any planned giving program is marketing. Planned giving is probably the only department in a development office that is likely to market. To stimulate business, the planned giving officer plays the role of the entrepreneur on behalf of the program. Without a strong marketing effort, most donors will not know about the giving opportunities offered by the organization. Use marketing vehicles to help prospects identify themselves to the organization, and over time the marketing effort will result in planned gifts for the organization.

## CHAPTER 2

Preparing Agreements

INTRODUCTION

Planned giving staff members regularly draft a variety of types of agreements to process planned gifts. These agreements govern endowed funds, current-use awards, chairs and professorships, life income gifts of real estate, and nontraditional assets, such as tangible personal property and gift annuities. Agreements outline the duties and responsibilities between the charity and the donor. This chapter examines a variety of types of agreements that are used by planned giving staff members.

DOCUMENTS

This chapter and the documents included in Section 2 of the CD-ROM focus exclusively on Agreements. The CD-ROM contains 50 documents that perform the functions described in this chapter. In addition the following documents are specifically referenced and included in this chapter:

Document 98	Current-Use Scholarship Award
Document 85	Agreement to Establish a Scholarship Umbrella Fund
Document 86	Endowment Agreement to Support Multiple Purposes
Document 89	The Presidential Excellence Endowment Fund
Document 101	Chair
Document 109	Two-Beneficiary Charitable Gift Annuity Agreement
Document 421	Instrument of Transfer
Document 117	Retained Life Estate
Document 124	Deed of Gift
Document 123	Curation Agreement for a Collection

ENDOWED NAMING OPPORTUNITIES

Endowed naming opportunities, such as endowed chairs, scholarships, or endowed funds, typically include planned giving as a funding mechanism. A printed list of endowed naming opportunities and their corresponding costs can help to raise a donor's philanthropic sights (see Exhibit 2-1). Some competitive donors see the higher-level endowed fund options as a challenge to be met. The price associated with the endowed fund and a fund's wide range of opportunities alert donors to the organization's needs and the cost to fund these needs.

 **EXHIBIT 2-1.**   SUMMARY OF ENDOWED NAMING OPPORTUNITY MINIMUMS

‹ORGANIZATION›

University Chair	‹ $ ›
Institute*	‹ $ ›
Center*	‹ $ ›
Professorship*	‹ $ ›
Visiting Lecture Series	‹ $ ›
Scholar-in-Residence	‹ $ ›
Full Tuition, Room and Board (In-State)	‹ $ ›
Graduate Fellowship	‹ $ ›
Full Tuition Scholarship (In-State)	‹ $ ›
Endowed Scholarship Fund	‹ $ ›

*Exact minimums depend on the scope of the project.

CREATING AN ENDOWED FUND

Although endowments may be established by outright gifts that do not involve planned giving, the use of planned giving vehicles commonly is associated with establishing or augmenting endowed funds, and a fund description must be prepared. An endowment is a gift arrangement established in perpetuity, through which the principal of the fund remains intact and only the income is paid out, most often on an annual basis. The principal is the amount of cash or property contributed by the donor, and the income is the earnings produced from the principal. Endowments may be established for any purpose and commonly are named after donors. Many donors establish named endowed memorial funds in memory of family members or friends. A named memorial gift fund becomes a lasting symbol of the bond between the organization and those who are forever honored and their families. A permanently endowed fund can benefit scholarships, academic programs, research, institutes, institutional or organizational programs, professorships and chairs, faculty support, exhibitions, or operations.

An endowed fund provides annual support to teaching, learning, and research each year in perpetuity. Endowed funds help support faculty projects, research programs, fellowships, exhibits, lecture series, athletic programs, and virtually any of the non-profit's departments. By creating an endowed fund, a donor makes a lasting contribution to the future of a nonprofit organization.

A donor can specify in writing the purposes that the endowed gift is to serve and how the fund is to be administered within the framework of the nonprofit's investment policies. Endowed funds can be created at any type of organization. A named fund can grow with the help of family and friends; often they make gifts to a family fund in lieu of birthday or holiday presents.

SCHOLARSHIP FUNDS

At educational institutions, teaching hospitals, and other organizations that offer a formal teaching component, endowed scholarship and fellowship funds provide much-needed financial assistance to worthy and financially needy students. Donors who create a scholarship fund must consider criteria to determine eligibility. They may opt to provide assistance to a student majoring in a specific field in a certain department or studying a particular subject. Donors may choose to provide scholarship assistance to a graduate or undergraduate student. They can establish criteria for the candidate's academic qualifications and financial need eligibility to receive the award.

FINANCING ENDOWED FUNDS

Donors also must decide how to meet the minimum funding level required at the organization that is establishing the fund. They may fund an endowed fund with cash, through a planned gift, or through a bequest from their estate. When a life income gift is used to fund an endowment, the remainder of the gift after the death of the life income beneficiary is available to fund the endowment. This is an important point because some people mistakenly believe that a life income gift is available at the time the gift is made. However, as with most planned gifts, the remainder is available only upon the death of the donor or beneficiary. Depending on the vehicle selected, the remainder value may be less than the initial gift. Therefore, some organizations prefer to use the value of the remainder interest rather than the value of the gift at the time the gift is made to determine whether a donor has contributed a sufficient sum to reach the endowed level. Another approach is to fully value the gift at the time of funding as long as the income stream is payable only to the grantor and to the grantor's spouse and not to a series of other income beneficiaries.

CURRENT-USE AWARDS

An alternative to an endowed fund is a current-use fund. Current-use funds are established to make an award in the year the gift is made (see Exhibit 2-2). These funds do not grow each year but provide current financial assistance to a recipient and are expended by the end of the year. At many organizations a donor can create a named current-use fund for as little as $1,000. This money is often used for books, supplies, operational expenses, or small specific projects. Since the fund exists for only a year, it is a good practice to draft a fund description to avoid confusion or conflict, although a description is not absolutely necessary.

EXHIBIT 2-2.   CURRENT-USE SCHOLARSHIP AWARD AGREEMENT

This document should be prepared for all awards of $1,000 or more or for situations where donors are considering making a series of annual gifts for current-use awards.

DOCUMENT 98

CURRENT-USE SCHOLARSHIP AWARD

‹DONOR› Current-Use Scholarship Award

‹DONOR› and ‹ORGANIZATION› hereby propose to establish the ‹DONOR› Current-Use Scholarship Award at ‹ORGANIZATION› in accordance with the wishes of the donor. The Award shall be supported by cash gifts made by ‹DONOR›.

The Award is defined and administered as follows:

The title of the Award shall be the ‹DONOR› Current-Use Scholarship Award. The fund shall be used in one year to support students majoring in ‹DEPARTMENT› at ‹ORGANIZATION›.

The scholarship shall be used to make an award of ‹ $ › to one or more students majoring in ‹MAJOR› who have attained an academic grade point average of ‹ # › or better and are eligible for financial aid. The Award shall be made in the year ‹YEAR›. The ‹DONOR› Current-Use Scholarship Award shall be awarded in future years contingent upon the donor making additional gifts to fund the Award. This fund may become permanently endowed through a gift from the ‹DONOR›'s estate at her death.

_____	_____
Date	‹DONOR›
_____	_____
Date	‹ORGANIZATION›

FUND DESCRIPTION

One of the most effective marketing tools in planned giving is the fund description. A personalized fund description is an excellent way to encourage a donor to consider giving at a higher level to a fund established in the donor's name or in the name of a loved one. In anticipation of meeting with a donor, predraft a fund description that benefits the donor's area of interest. The donor is involved in the process from the beginning and feels closer to the organization. Explain to the donor how the money will be used and review any restrictions as to who will benefit from the gift. Donors often enjoy seeing their names associated with a program at the organization. The gratification of establishing an endowed fund is similar to that of having a wing of a building or room named in one's honor, but on a smaller financial scale.

The appendix and the CD-ROM include a number of standard fund description forms used to create an endowed fund in a donor's name. The forms can be modified to reflect the donor's interests and objectives. Each donor who inquires about establishing a fund should be provided with a fund description prepared by the nonprofit that includes a statement about the fund's purpose, a brief biographical sketch about the donor, and a distribution clause for paying income or principal to recipients. No other document is more persuasive or beneficial to a donor who is considering making a gift. A fund description helps close gifts.

Draft

When meeting with prospective donors, bring a draft of a fund description to the meeting. Prior to the meeting, fill in the donor's name and any information known about him or her. Create the fund in an area in which donors have expressed an interest. Present the fund description to them while explaining that they may wish to establish a fund to help financially needy students or support a specific program of interest that has continuing needs each year. Remind donors that the document is a draft that can easily be changed to incorporate specific ideas or needs. Stamp the word "draft" on the document. Donors who have the capacity often establish a fund in their name with cash rather than through a planned gift or bequest. Personalized fund descriptions are excellent development vehicles to convert development prospects into donors.

Selection of Recipient

Donors sometimes wish to be involved in the selection of recipients for endowed funds. A donor who makes a gift to a nonprofit and claims a charitable income tax deduction cannot be the sole decision maker in the selection of the recipient. The donor may, however, serve as a member of the selection committee composed of the organization's representatives. If the donor were to select the individual who received the financial benefit, the donor's charitable income tax deduction would be in jeopardy because in effect the donor would be paying tuition. As every parent soon learns, there is no charitable income tax deduction for tuition payments.

Restrictions

Nonprofits should avoid situations where a donor wishes to place restrictions excluding members of an ethnic or racial group from benefiting from an endowed fund. These restrictions are discriminatory, and if a restriction calls for excluding a member of a minority group, it is potentially illegal. Donors and nonprofits also should avoid using overly restrictive language that may prevent a recipient from being selected. Instead, restrictions should be expressed in the form of preferences.

MECHANICS OF AN ENDOWED FUND DESCRIPTION

For every endowed fund, an agreement is created between the donor and the non-profit. The agreement defines the obligations and the duties of both the donor in funding the gift and the nonprofit in making an award, selecting a recipient, and managing the principal of the fund. Typically a development or planned giving officer and the donor discuss how to create the fund. The minimum level to establish a named endowed fund at many organizations is $10,000, although it can be as high as $50,000 or more. A donor may fund it outright with cash or fund it partially or completely through a planned gift or through a bequest in his or her estate. If the fund is established while the donor is alive, then the donor can be recognized for establishing it and will perhaps have the chance to meet a fund recipient.

What should a fund description look like? It should be no more than one or two pages long. Be sure to have signature and date lines at the bottom. In addition:

- *Title the fund description after the donor:* The Diana Smith Endowed Scholarship Fund at (name of organization). Donors respond to recognition and enjoy seeing their names, family names, or the names of loved ones included in the title.

- *State the names of the parties creating the fund.* Generally this will include one or more donors and the name of the organization: "XYZ University and Miss Diana Smith hereby propose to establish The Diana Smith Endowed Scholarship Fund at XYZ University."

- *Describe how the fund shall be established financially,* such as through a bequest, a current gift, or a combination of both. This sentence enables the planned giving officer to discuss with the donor how the scholarship will be funded. Include language that permits additional gifts to be made to the fund.

- *Include a short background sketch of the donor(s).* State their relationship with the organization and, if appropriate, some of their outstanding achievements. Donors enjoy including this information because it helps a recipient to know something about the benefactors and serves as a permanent memorial to donors at their death.

- *State the fund's purpose.* For example: "The income of the fund shall be awarded to a graduate student at The School of Medicine who wishes to study gerontology." Most often a fund's purpose represents the donor's interests.

- *Describe how the fund will be administered financially.* For example, will the income be awarded on an annual basis? Will some of the income be returned to principal?

State whether the principal can be invaded to make an award. Can income generated be accumulated for future use or be returned to principal if an award is not made in a particular year? Explain the organization's investment policy to the donor.

- *State any restrictions.* For example, must the recipient be financially needy or academically worthy, or have attained a particular grade point average? Are there geographical requirements for recipients? Should recipients focus on a particular area of study? Again, most restrictions reflect a donor's interests. Strive to keep the fund limitations from becoming so restrictive that the organization is unable to award the scholarship each year because of an inadequate pool of eligible candidates.

- *Tell the donor how the recipient will be selected.* Will a committee composed of different representatives be used? Refer to committee representatives by title. Do not use specific individuals' names in the fund description in case the individual no longer wishes to serve or leaves the organization. The language may be similar to "Selection of candidates shall be made by the Office of Financial Aid in consultation with the Dean of the College of Liberal Arts." Remember that donors are prohibited from selecting the recipient by themselves.

- *Include a standard default clause* to protect the organization if in the future it is unable to fulfill the terms of the fund. The clause may read: "If it becomes impossible to accomplish the purposes of this gift, the income or principal, or both, shall be used for scholarships in such manner as determined by the Board of Trustees of (name of organization)." This language can frustrate many donors. Assure them that the language is used to protect their gift in case the school, program, or department they wish to benefit ceases to exist. If a donor will not sign the description if the language is included, strike the language and accommodate the donor's wishes.

- *Include a statement requiring that a specific governing board approve of the fund.* For example: "The establishment of this fund is subject to the approval of (name of organization's) Gift Review Committee." This statement enables the committee to review the fund description and determine the legalities of any restrictions.

- *Encourage the donor to get involved in the drafting process.* Involving the donor now ultimately benefits the organization and the donor. Be creative in drafting the initial fund description. Based on the organization's giving minimums and the donor's potential, decide if the fund is an endowed fund or a current-use fund.

- *Present new donors with a variety of options at different funding levels.*

FUND DESCRIPTIONS FOR SPECIFIC PURPOSES

Endowed funds also are used to provide support to more than one of the nonprofit's programs or departments. Exhibits 2-3 through 2-6 are agreements that enable donors to direct funding to different programs. Donors simply may allocate percentages of income among the fund's objectives. Agreements also are used to establish endowed chairs and professorships. The exhibits include an endowed chair description.

Many wealthy donors who are involved closely with a nonprofit prefer to fund a number of the charity's departments. In this example, the agreement provides donors with opportunities to allocate income to four departments. This agreement is appropriate for a donor who has multiple interests at a charity.

DOCUMENT 85

AGREEMENT TO ESTABLISH A SCHOLARSHIP UMBRELLA FUND

‹NAME OF FUND› Endowment
‹ORGANIZATION›

‹DONORS› and the ‹ORGANIZATION› hereby propose to establish the ‹FUND› at ‹ORGANIZATION› in accordance with the wishes of the donors. The endowment was funded through a gift of ‹ $ › from ‹DONORS›.

The fund is defined and administered as follows:

The income will be used to support the following ‹ORGANIZATION› departments in the percentages indicated. The income is to be used at the discretion of the respective department heads.

_____% Department of _____

_____% Department of _____

_____% Department of _____

_____% Department of _____

_____	_____
Date	‹DONOR›
_____	_____
Date	‹DONOR›
_____	_____
Date	‹NAME› ‹TITLE›

EXHIBIT 2-4.   ENDOWMENT AGREEMENT

This agreement can be used to support several initiatives within one department or program at a charity. The purposes and percentages can be modified to meet the needs of the donor and the charity.

DOCUMENT 86

ENDOWMENT AGREEMENT TO SUPPORT MULTIPLE PURPOSES
The ‹DONOR› Family Endowment Fund
‹ORGANIZATION›

‹DONOR› and the ‹ORGANIZATION› hereby propose to establish the ‹DONOR› Endowment Fund at ‹ORGANIZATION›. The endowment shall be funded through a gift from ‹DONOR›, and additional gifts may be made by ‹DONOR› family members, friends, and ‹LOCAL ORGANIZATIONS›.

The fund is defined and administered as follows:

The title of the fund shall be the ‹FUND TITLE›. The earnings shall be used to support the following purposes in the percentages indicated:

1. **‹SCHOLARSHIPS›:** ‹ % › shall be distributed to support honors scholarships at the ‹DEPARTMENT OR PROGRAM› for students from ‹NAME› County who have grade point averages of 3.5 or better who are interested in pursuing careers in ‹DEPARTMENT›.

2. **‹INSTITUTE›:** ‹ % › shall be distributed to support the ‹NAME› Institute at the ‹DEPARTMENT›.

3. **‹PROFESSORSHIP›:** ‹ % › shall be distributed for the purpose of supporting an endowed professorship in ‹FIELD›.

4. **‹CONFERENCES›:** ‹ % › shall be distributed for the purpose of conducting lecture-ships, seminars, and conferences promoting ‹DESCRIPTION›.

If the purpose of the fund cannot reasonably be achieved, then the fund shall be used to establish an endowed fund for ‹DESCRIPTION›. Note: Alternatively, the fund shall be used in accordance with the stated intentions of the donors in the discretion of the Board of Trustees of ‹ORGANIZATION›.

Date	‹DONOR›
Date	‹DONOR›
Date	‹NAME› ‹TITLE›

EXHIBIT 2-5.   THE PRESIDENTIAL EXCELLENCE
ENDOWMENT FUND AGREEMENT

Most agreements are very specific. However, this agreement provides complete
discretion to the charity's president to determine the use of the income from
the gift. This document promotes excellence through an unrestricted gift.

DOCUMENT 89

THE PRESIDENTIAL EXCELLENCE ENDOWMENT FUND

The <DONOR NAME> Presidential Excellence Fund
<ORGANIZATION>

<DONOR> and the <ORGANIZATION> hereby propose to establish the <FUND NAME> at <ORGA-
NIZATION> in accordance with the wishes of the donor. The endowment shall be funded
through a gift from the estate of <DONOR> in memory of <NAME>.

The fund is defined and administered as follows:

The title of the fund shall be the <FUND NAME> Presidential Excellence Fund. Proceeds from
the estate of <DONOR> will support this fund. The fund is an unrestricted fund allowing the
income to be used at the discretion of the President in furtherance of the mission of <ORGA-
NIZATION>.

If the purpose of the fund cannot reasonably be achieved, then the fund shall be used to
establish an endowed fund for <DESCRIPTION>. (Note: Alternatively, the fund shall be used
in accordance with the stated intentions of the donors in the discretion of the Board of
Trustees of <ORGANIZATION>).

Date	<DONOR>
Date	<DONOR>
Date	<DONOR>
	<TITLE>

EXHIBIT 2-6.   CHAIR AGREEMENT

Chair fund descriptions describe criteria for the use of the chair. Criteria can
include the holder's eligibility, duration, selection, scope, and purpose.
This document establishes a chair in law and business and provides salary,
staff support, and expenses associated with the chair to the holder of the
chair. The donor establishes this chair through a bequest.

EXHIBIT 2-6. CHAIR AGREEMENT *(Continued)*

DOCUMENT 101

FUND DESCRIPTION FOR A CHAIR

The ‹DONOR› Chair
in Entrepreneurial Law and Business
at
‹ORGANIZATION›

We hereby propose to establish the ‹DONOR› Chair in Law and Business at ‹ORGANIZATION›. ‹DONOR› is a graduate of the ‹DEPARTMENT/COLLEGE› and chairman of ‹COMPANY NAME›. The Chair is to be funded by a gift from ‹DONOR›'s estate equal to the funding level necessary to establish a chair at the time of ‹DONOR›'s death. The current level to establish a chair is ‹ $ ›.

The title of the Chair shall be the ‹DONOR› Chair in Law and Business. The income from this bequest shall be used to provide support to the holder of the Chair in the form of salary, staff support, and other expenses associated with the Chair. The Chair will be dedicated to the promotion and exploration of the relationship between law and business from the perspective of the entrepreneur. To select the holder of the Chair, the dean of the School of Law shall appoint a search committee composed of three members of the Law School faculty, one School of Management faculty member, and a business entrepreneur. The search committee will identify and interview candidates and recommend to the law faculty the best-qualified person to fill the Chair. The dean of the School of Law shall recommend the appointment of the candidates to ‹ORGANIZATION›.

Entrepreneurs are a driving force in industrial progress, the cutting edge of business progress. At the same time, their risks are high. Probability of failure is ever present, bringing with it possible loss of the entrepreneur's livelihood. The Chair is established for the purpose of improving the legal system's understanding and support for enterprising risk-takers and for those who reflect the vision and creativity of ‹DONOR›. It is also established for the purpose of encouraging entrepreneurship by improving the legal services that entrepreneurs receive and, therefore, the business climate itself.

The Chair shall be devoted to the relationship of law and business, including scholarship and teaching in the areas of business formation, organization, corporate reorganization, financing, and the raising of capital. The Chair shall consider the impact of trade, and other governmental regulation, corporate taxation, intellectual property, merger and transfer of business organizations, state-of-the-art business operations, and practical considerations in business management.

In addition to the study of substantive issues in business and law, the holder of the Chair shall promote and foster an awareness of the attorney's role in dealing with an entrepreneur

---

EXHIBIT 2-6.   CHAIR AGREEMENT *(Continued)*

---

as a special business client. The holder of the ‹DONOR› Chair in Law and Business shall teach courses in one or more of the following fields: corporations, economic regulation of business, antitrust law, securities law, corporate reorganization, corporate finance, and taxation.

If in the judgment of trustees of ‹ORGANIZATION› it becomes impossible to accomplish the purposes of this gift, the income or principal, or both, may be used in such manner as determined by trustees of ‹ORGANIZATION›.

Date	‹DONOR›
Date	For ‹ORGANIZATION›: ‹NAME›, ‹TITLE›

LIFE INCOME GIFT AGREEMENTS

Planned giving staff members regularly prepare a variety of agreements associated with life income gifts. Most of these agreements are contractual in nature, enabling donors to transfer cash or property to the charity and, in exchange, to receive an income stream. The most common life income gifts are charitable gift annuities, deferred gift annuities, and gifts to a pooled income fund. Because charitable gift annuities and deferred gift annuities are similar, they will be discussed together.

Charitable Gift Annuities and Deferred Gift Annuities

For charitable gift annuities and deferred gift annuities, the charity prepares a gift agreement that contains information about the donor and the gift. The agreement lists the donor's name, address, and social security number; documents the timing of payments, amount of payments, partial payments (if any); and designates the balance of the principal of the gift at the time of the beneficiary's death (see Exhibit 2-7). The designation of the principal typically is included in the annuity agreement, for simplicity's sake, although it may be made through a separate distribution agreement.

Pooled Income Funds

Pooled income funds use a specific document, called an instrument of transfer, to transfer assets from a donor to the charity. In addition, each donor must be presented with a pooled income fund prospectus prior to executing an instrument of transfer. Once donors have made the first gift to the fund, they make additional gifts by using a subsequent gift agreement form (see Exhibit 2-8).

EXHIBIT 2-7.   TWO-BENEFICIARY GIFT ANNUITY AGREEMENT

This is a two-beneficiary gift annuity agreement that distributes the principal of the gift. **Note:** Local practice varies state to state, so this agreement should be reviewed by the charity's general counsel or legal advisor.

DOCUMENT 109

TWO-BENEFICIARY CHARITABLE
GIFT ANNUITY AGREEMENT

‹ORGANIZATION›, a charitable corporation located in ‹CITY, STATE›, agrees to pay to ‹DONOR›, of ‹CITY, STATE› (hereinafter called the "Donor"), for the Donor's life and thereafter to the Donor's spouse, ‹SPOUSE'S NAME›, for ‹HIS/HER› life if ‹HE/SHE› survives the Donor, an annuity in the annual sum of ‹AMOUNT IN WORDS›, (‹DOLLAR AMOUNT›) from the date hereof, in equal quarterly installments of ‹ $ › on the last day of March, June, September, and December; provided, however, that the Donor may, by the Donor's last will, revoke the annuity to be paid to the Donor's said spouse. The first installment shall be payable on ‹DATE›. This annuity shall be nonassignable, except in the case of a voluntary transfer of part or all of such annuity to ‹ORGANIZATION›.

The obligation of ‹ORGANIZATION› to make annuity payments shall terminate with the payment preceding the death of the survivor of the Donor and the Donor's said spouse, unless the Donor revokes the annuity payable to the Donor's said spouse, in which case ‹ORGANIZATION›'s obligation shall terminate with the payment preceding the death of the Donor.

‹ORGANIZATION› certifies that the Donor, as an evidence of the Donor's desire to support the work of ‹ORGANIZATION› and to make a charitable gift, has this day contributed to ‹ORGANIZATION› the property listed in Schedule A attached hereto, receipt of which is acknowledged for its general charitable purposes.

IN WITNESS WHEREOF, ‹ORGANIZATION› has executed this instrument this day of

_____, 20_____.

_____
‹ORGANIZATION›

_____
‹NAME›

_____
‹TITLE›

EXHIBIT 2-8.   INSTRUMENT OF TRANSFER AGREEMENT

This instrument of transfer enables the donor to transfer cash or stock to the pooled income fund. Pooled income fund administrators typically provide participating clients with copies of these documents. This instrument of transfer also appears in Chapter 7.

DOCUMENT 421

POOLED INCOME FUND INSTRUMENT OF TRANSFER

IRS Form: Rev. Proc. 88-53

SECTION 5. Sample Instrument of Transfer: One Life

On this ‹***› day of ‹***›, 20‹***›, I hereby transfer to the ‹***› Public Charity Pooled Income Fund, under the terms and conditions set forth in its Declaration of Trust, the following property: ‹***›.

The income interest attributable to the property transferred shall be paid as follows:

A. To me during my lifetime.

B. To ‹***› during his or her life. However, I reserve the right to revoke, solely by will, this income interest.

Upon the termination of the income interest, the Trustee of the Fund will sever from the Fund an amount equal to the value of the remainder interest in the transferred property and transfer it to Public Charity:

A. For its general uses and purposes.

B. For the following charitable purpose(s): ‹***›. However, if it is not possible for Public Charity in its sole discretion to use the severed amount for the specified purpose(s), then it may be used for the general purposes of Public Charity. This instrument and the transfer of property made pursuant thereto shall be effective after acceptance by both Donor and the Trustee.

IN WITNESS WHEREOF ‹***› and ‹TRUSTEE› by its duly authorized officer have signed this agreement the day and year first above written.

_____

‹DONOR›

_____

‹TRUSTEE›

By _____

‹ACKNOWLEDGMENTS, WITNESSES, ETC.›

REAL ESTATE

Charities prepare a number of real estate agreements regarding gifts of real estate (see Exhibit 2-9). Many real estate agreements are recorded at the local registry of deeds, and each region has particular requirements for recording. Because local law governs many of the agreements, such as deeds, legal counsel knowledgeable in real estate law should prepare retained life estate contracts and all real estate contracts.

EXHIBIT 2-9.   RETAINED LIFE ESTATE

This document describes a gift of real estate through which the donor retains a life estate. As discussed in the text, the document should be prepared by legal counsel experienced in real estate law.

DOCUMENT 117

RETAINED LIFE ESTATE AGREEMENT

THIS AGREEMENT entered into this _____ day of _____, 20 _____ by and between ‹ORGANIZATION› and ‹DONOR› of _____, ‹STREET, CITY, STATE› (the "Grantor").

WITNESSETH THAT:

WHEREAS, the Grantor has this day executed a deed giving to ‹ORGANIZATION› a remainder interest in ‹HIS/HER› personal residence located at ‹STREET, CITY, STATE› (the "Property"),
NOW, THEREFORE, the parties hereto agree as follows:

1. The Grantor shall, during ‹HIS/HER› lifetime, have the sole right to occupy and utilize the premises as ‹HIS/HER› residence and to lease the premises to any other person for use as a personal residence.

2. ‹ORGANIZATION› shall join in any lease of the premises to another in order to permit the lease term to continue beyond the death of the Grantor, provided that such term shall not continue for more than one year beyond the date of death of the Grantor and provided further that ‹ORGANIZATION› shall be entitled to the rent from the property from the date of death of the Grantor.

3. The Grantor shall have the sole responsibility for maintaining the property, paying real estate taxes, insuring the property against loss and liability, and shall not, without the consent of ‹ORGANIZATION›, suffer any lien or mortgage to be placed on the property other than liens or mortgages which may now exist, and shall not, without the consent of ‹ORGANIZATION›, permit the amount of any lien or mortgage now existing to increase.

EXHIBIT 2-9.   RETAINED LIFE ESTATE *(Continued)*

---

4. In the event of any damage to the property, the Grantor, at ‹HIS/HER› sole expense, shall cause such damage to be repaired unless the Grantor and ‹ORGANIZATION› shall agree that it is impractical to do so, in which case, any insurance proceeds resulting from such damage shall be divided between ‹ORGANIZATION› and the Grantor in accordance with the value of their respective interests as of the date such damage occurred. For purposes of determining the value of ‹ORGANIZATION›'s interest in the event of such loss, the value shall be determined in the same manner as is used to value a gift of a remainder interest in a personal residence or a farm as is provided in U.S. Treasury Regulation (Section) 1.170A-12 or any corresponding U.S. Treasury Regulations then in effect, using the rate of interest determined under IRC (Section) 7520 in effect for the month in which the loss occurred.

5. The Grantor agrees to hold ‹ORGANIZATION› harmless against any and all liability arising from the property during the lifetime of the Grantor.

6. The Grantor may at any time or times at ‹HIS/HER› sole expense make improvements to the property, provided that such improvements shall not result in a reduction of the value of the property.

IN WITNESS WHEREOF, the parties hereto have set their hands and seals the day and year first above written.

For: ‹ORGANIZATION›

By: ‹NAME›, ‹TITLE›

‹NAME›, Grantor

NONTRADITIONAL ASSETS

Nontraditional assets include tangible personal property, collections and collectibles, gifts of inventory, and other types of assets. Specific procedures exist to transfer each of these assets from the donor to the charity. For example, tangible personal property often is transferred by a deed of gift. This agreement transfers the donor's interest in the property to a charity and provides certain assurances that the donor is in fact the owner of the property. Once the property is transferred and is in the hands of the charity, additional agreements may be needed that govern the use of the property. For example, a curation agreement outlines the duties and obligations of the donor and the charity with respect to a gift of a collection (see Exhibits 2-10 and 2-11).

EXHIBIT 2-10. Deed of Gift Agreement

This is a sample deed of gift form. Like all legal agreements, it should be prepared or reviewed by competent legal counsel.

DOCUMENT 124

DEED OF GIFT
‹ORGANIZATION›

DONOR: _____
             Name(s)

ADDRESS: _____
             Street

               _____
             City, State Zip

I /We, ‹NAME OF DONOR(S)›, represent and guarantee that I/we is/are the lawful owners of the property described below, that it is free of all encumbrances, and that I/we have the right to give or transfer legal title to the following property to ‹ORGANIZATION›:
‹ADD DESCRIPTION OF PROPERTY›
I (We) declare the appraised value of the above listed property(s) on this date as $_____.

_____   _____
Donor Signature   Date   Donor Signature   Date

STATE OF _____, COUNTY OF _____

The foregoing instrument was acknowledged before me this ____ day of _____, 20__.

My commission expires: _____   _____
                                       NOTARY PUBLIC

ACCEPTANCE OF GIFT

_____ on behalf of ‹ORGANIZATION›, accept the legal title of the gift from ‹NAME OF DONOR(S)›, donor(s), of the above described property.

_____   _____
Signature   Title   Date

STATE OF _____, COUNTY OF _____

The foregoing instrument was acknowledged before me this ____ day of _____, 20__.

My commission expires: _____   _____
                                       NOTARY PUBLIC

EXHIBIT 2-11.	CURATION AGREEMENT FOR A COLLECTION

This curation agreement governs arrangements for the transfer, management, display, and storage of a collection of tangible personal property. It addresses the appointment of a curator, publicity, location of the collection, and conditions.

DOCUMENT 123

MEMORANDUM OF UNDERSTANDING REGARDING COLLECTION

‹DONORS› and ‹ORGANIZATION› hereby agree to enter into a curation agreement for the ‹DONORS› gift of ‹NAME OF› collection to ‹ORGANIZATION›. This curation agreement outlines responsibilities of ‹ORGANIZATION› in accepting the gift and defines the arrangements for the transfer, management, display, and storage of the collection.

Description of Collection

The collection consists of ‹PROVIDE GENERAL DESCRIPTION OF THE COLLECTION›. In particular, the collection contains ‹NUMBER, COLOR, TYPE OF PROPERTY CONTRIBUTED IN THE COLLECTION›. Each piece of the collection has been inventoried and assigned an inventory number that is located in a catalog. A copy of the catalog is attached to this agreement and is incorporated by reference.

Curator

‹NAME, TITLE› shall be appointed curator of the collection on behalf of ‹ORGANIZATION›. The curator shall be responsible for ‹DESCRIBE DUTIES OF CURATOR› and for maintaining inventory control on each item in the collection and shall provide an annual report to the donors detailing the location of each piece of the collection.

Selection Committee

A selection committee will be organized and once organized will be responsible for selecting pieces for display and for developing a system to restore the collection so that each piece will be on display at least ‹NUMBER› years out of ‹NUMBER›. The committee will consist of ‹NUMBER› members and shall include two representatives of the donors and three representatives of ‹ORGANIZATION›.

Initial Funding for Expenses

The cost of cataloging, labeling, transferring, maintenance, display, and storage shall be underwritten by the donors who have provided ‹ $ › to cover these expenses. The donors shall receive an annual accounting on the status of the account. The donors agree to provide additional funding during their lifetimes if the original amount is depleted.

EXHIBIT 2-11.   CURATION AGREEMENT FOR A COLLECTION *(Continued)*

Permanent Funding for the Collection

The donors and ‹ORGANIZATION› have agreed to establish an endowed fund to provide permanent support for the collection with funding provided by the donor in the amount of ‹ $ ›. A copy of the endowment agreement is attached and is incorporated by reference to this agreement.

Publicity/Brochures

The curator, in consultation with the selection committee, shall draft a press release and other forms of communication regarding the collection. In addition, the curator shall prepare a brochure so that visitors and guests of ‹ORGANIZATION› will learn about the collection.

Management of the Collection

The curator shall prepare and manage the collection. The collection shall be maintained in its entirety and during the lifetime of the donors, ‹ORGANIZATION› will not sell, trade, or loan any piece of the collection without the approval of the donors. Upon the death of the donors, the committee will not sell, trade, or loan any piece of the collection without the approval of the selection committee.

Location

It is the intent of the donors that the collection be located in the ‹LOCATION› of the ‹NAME› building for a period of ‹NUMBER › years. After this period, the collection will not be moved without the approval of the selection committee.

Relocation

Should ‹ORGANIZATION› determine that the collection be relocated, ‹ORGANIZATION› can do so only if all of the following conditions are met:

1. The new space is equal to the square footage of the previous space.
2. The new building housing the collection is more specifically related to the collection than the previous building.
3. The donors consent to the relocation during their lifetime, or if the proposed relocation occurs following their deaths, their designee approves the move.
4. Describe other conditions.

Deaccessioning

The collection will be maintained in perpetuity. The collection can only be deaccessioned if the following conditions are met: ‹DESCRIBE CONDITIONS›

Date

‹DONOR›

Date

‹ORGANIZATION REPRESENTATIVE›

CONCLUSION

Nonprofit organizations receive significant financial support through planned giving arrangements. These arrangements require agreements to protect the interests of both the charity and the donor. The agreements should define the obligations of each party. Carefully prepared agreements prevent misunderstandings and simplify the gift process. The donors of these funds and their families are permanently linked to the nonprofit organization. The fund description protects the interests of the donors and defines the obligations of the nonprofit organization.

## CHAPTER 3

Correspondence

INTRODUCTION

Correspondence consists of two major types of documents:

1. Letters
2. Memoranda (memos)

Generally, letters are a more formal type of document in terms of format, although the contents of a letter can be either formal or informal. Letters are sent to audiences outside of the workplace while memos are sent within the workplace to other employees. Memos also may be sent to vendors, suppliers, or businesses that provide a product or service to the nonprofit organization.

Correspondence accomplishes one or more of the following objectives:

- Opens a new line of communication with prospects
- Maintains a line of communication with existing donors
- Records details, facts, and financial information about planned gifts
- Summarizes detailed information
- Asks for specific action
- Requests information
- Attempts to persuade donors or prospects to make gifts
- Explains planned giving concepts
- Educates readers about gift options
- Provides a rationale for decision making

Correspondence may be mailed or transmitted electronically through e-mail. Each transmission method has advantages and disadvantages. Consider the likely preferences of the reader when choosing one form over the other. Some donors clearly prefer e-mail while others respond better to mailed correspondence. For very important cor-respondence, even when donors regularly communicate using e-mail, it is a good idea to send a hard copy after the e-mail. Correspondence, printed on letterhead and mailed, has more of an official tone than e-mail.

Documents

This chapter and the documents included in Section 3 of the CD-ROM focus exclu-sively on Correspondence. The CD-ROM contains 114 documents that perform the functions described in this chapter. In addition the following documents are specifi-cally referenced and included in this chapter:

Document 143	Gift Annuity/Pooled Income Fund Comparison
Document 219	Response to Donor Clarifying Role of Organization When Project Is Beyond Scope of Organization
Document 218	Follow-Up Meeting to Discuss Charitable Gift Planning
Document 206	Follow-Up on Request for Information
Document 158	Proposal to Donor Explaining Gift of Stock
Document 196	Information for Fund Description
Document 230	Ambassador Program
Document 214	Letter to Donor at End of Year

Preparation

Writing effective forms of correspondence requires careful preparation. To write well, the writer must carefully consider the:

- Purpose of the correspondence
- Needs of the reader
- Depth (extent) of the writing

Considering these questions adequately prepares the writer to develop effective doc-uments.

Purpose

The document's purpose may be to encourage the reader to take action, such as sign an agreement, write a check, or make a transfer of appreciated securities. Often the purpose is clearly stated in the opening paragraph; however, the purpose also may be subtle, depending on the parties involved, their relationship, and the nature (reasons) of the writing (see Exhibit 3-1).

EXHIBIT 3-1.   GIFT ANNUITY/POOLED INCOME FUND COMPARISON LETTER

This letter shows the differences between a gift to a pooled income fund and a charitable gift annuity. The letter objectively explains the benefits of each and then summarizes the benefits for the donor. The letter was written immediately following a telephone conversation to confirm the substance of it.

DOCUMENT 143

GIFT ANNUITY/POOLED INCOME FUND COMPARISON

Dear ‹NAME›:

It was nice to speak with you yesterday regarding your gift to benefit ‹ORGANIZATION›. You mentioned that you would be interested in information about life income gift options such as a charitable gift annuity or a pooled income fund. The following are the benefits of each:

A charitable gift annuity is a contract between you and ‹ORGANIZATION›. You and your wife receive a fixed dollar amount each year for your lifetimes. The charitable gift annuity is based on the size of the gift and your ages at the time your gift is made. For donors ages ‹AGE› and ‹AGE›, who make a ‹ $ › gift, the annuity rate is ‹ % ›, which provides an annual income of ‹ $ ›. In addition, you receive an immediate charitable income tax deduction of ‹ $ ›. This deduction can be taken in the year the gift is made, or if necessary, it can be used for five additional years.

The pooled income fund works much like a mutual fund. A gift is made to the fund and it, in turn, pays out interest quarterly to the donors for your lifetimes. The rate is variable and currently pays ‹ % ›. A gift of ‹ $ › by donors ages ‹AGE› and ‹AGE› provides an income of ‹ $ › each year, assuming a constant rate of return. The charitable income tax deduction is ‹ $ ›. An additional advantage to the pooled income fund is that it can be funded with appreciated securities and the donors incur no capital gains taxes.

The charitable gift annuity offers you a slightly ‹HIGHER or LOWER› income, some of which is tax-free income, but a ‹LARGER or GREATER› charitable income tax deduction than the pooled income fund. However, the pooled income fund avoids capital gains taxes. You may wish to select the option based on your needs or consult with a financial advisor.

Thank you for your interest in ‹ORGANIZATION›. If you have any questions, please call me at ‹TELEPHONE›. I look forward to hearing from you.

Reader

When documents are drafted, often the person most overlooked is the reader. Most writers fail to consider the reader's role in the document. Who is the reader, a planned giving donor or a new prospect? What role does he or she play? How well does the writer know the reader? Is the document being sent to a single individual, or is it part of a general mailing? Does the information pertain to a specific individual, or is it generic? How much does the reader know about the nonprofit organization? Its purposes? Programs? Services? Mission? Staff? Charitable gift programs? History? Resources? Needs? How much experience does the reader have in charitable giving? How familiar is the reader with the subject of the document? How much must be explained? Will the document be in context for the reader, or will it need to be placed in context or require background information?

All documents must take readers' needs into consideration. The best documents quietly let readers know that the writer has done just that. The document must be thoughtful, helpful, and provide the right amount of background, history, and explanation (see Exhibit 3-2). As a result, readers will find the document easy to read and in context, and know that it is responsive to their needs even if the information is not what they want to hear, as is the case with this next letter.

EXHIBIT 3-2.   RESPONSE TO DONOR CLARIFYING ROLE OF ORGANIZATION

In a previous letter, a donor asked a nonprofit organization to start a project that is beyond the organization's scope. The donor is willing to provide partial funding. Here the author is responding to the donor's request. This carefully worded response takes care to not alienate the donor even though the nonprofit organization will not be able to meet the donor's needs. The letter provides more than an answer; it educates the donor about the decision and the reasons for it.

DOCUMENT 219

RESPONSE TO DONOR CLARIFYING ROLE OF ORGANIZATION WHEN PROJECT IS BEYOND ORGANIZATION'S SCOPE

Dear <NAME>:

It was wonderful to see you both at <EVENT>. We are honored that you participated in our <EVENT> and we hope that you enjoyed your time at <ORGANIZATION>.

EXHIBIT 3-2.   RESPONSE TO DONOR CLARIFYING ROLE
OF ORGANIZATION *(Continued)*

We very much appreciate your interest in supporting ‹ORGANIZATION› and we share your concerns. ‹ORGANIZATION› is a national leader in providing educational access and opportunities for ‹_____› students. The issues we face on campus in supporting our ‹_____› student population are the very issues that you have addressed in your proposal and in our joint conversations. The purpose of this letter is to outline those areas where (1) we feel we can have a direct impact, (2) we feel we can indirectly influence initiatives, and (3) there are initiatives beyond the scope of what ‹ORGANIZATION› is capable of doing.

1. ‹ORGANIZATION› can have a direct impact on the following initiatives:

   • Coordinate campus activities among ‹_____›-sponsored organizations.

   • Invite prominent ‹_____› leaders to speak, organize community outreach programs.

   • Coordinate educational programming with the public schools.

   • Coordinate internships for ‹_____› students.

   • Promote fund-raising efforts that support ‹_____› issues.

2. ‹ORGANIZATION› can indirectly influence the following initiatives:

   • Coordinate outreach efforts to educate ‹_____› about educational opportunities and access.

   • Coordinate and develop relations between the campus and business professionals in the community.

   • Coordinate outreach efforts to educate ‹_____› students about social and economic issues.

Before we discuss those initiatives that we believe are beyond our scope, I want to explain the way we make decisions about what we can and cannot do. Our decisions are restricted in that we may pursue only initiatives that fulfill the mission of ‹ORGANIZATION›. Many of our choices are dictated to us by the ‹GOVERNING BOARD› and by the grant of authority that the Internal Revenue Service gives us as a charitable organization. The State and the IRS prevent us from engaging in political or legislative agendas. We cannot, for example, engage in the political process or become advocates on behalf of ‹_____› or any single group. The scope of our work excludes our ability to serve as a political action group in arenas such as ‹DESCRIBE›.

Enclosed is a summary of the programs, departments, agencies, and entities in our educational community that address the academic and social needs of ‹_____› and their families. The listing shows that our extended community has extraordinary resources and commitment to improve the lives of ‹_____› in our service area. ‹ORGANIZATION› is in

---

---

a position to help these programs in direct and indirect ways to articulate a unified vision, develop coordinated work plans, implement rigorous programs, and resolve historically difficult problems.

Starting a new program, such as the one you envision, is an expensive undertaking. We also would not want to engage in a new venture if we did not feel we would be successful. We know you would not want us to undertake such a substantial effort without adequate funding, since to do so would doom the project. Because ‹ORGANIZATION›'s budget is linked to specific line items, we do not have discretionary funds to be used in support of all the initiatives that you propose. We have revised our budget and enclosed a copy for your review. For us to move forward, we need a minimum budget of $200,000 that will be provided exclusively by outside funding. This budget would enable us to study, develop, and implement a series of initiatives that would meet your objectives, make a difference to the ‹_____› community, and, it is hoped, serve as a national model.

We hope to fulfill the objective, stated so well in your letter, of establishing an institute for learning, one that brings together the community, the public schools, and ‹ORGANIZA-TION›. With your support, ‹ORGANIZATION› will develop the ‹DONOR NAME› Institute at ‹ORGANIZATION›. By the end of one year, the ‹DONOR NAME› Institute will have hosted a major conference on ‹_____› Issues in Education, inaugurated a speaker's series, established relationships with the business and professional community, expanded intern-ship opportunities statewide, and activated a network of community partners who share your vision. You will, of course, be invited to open the conference and introduce the speaker.

I welcome the opportunity to discuss this matter further. I can be reached at ‹TELE-PHONE›. I look forward to meeting with you and discussing ways in which we can meet your needs, together with the needs of ‹ORGANIZATION›.

> Sincerely,
>
> ‹NAME›

Enclosure: ‹BUDGET›

Scope

Once the purpose of the writing is clearly defined and readers are identified, the writer must address the scope of the writing. Scope refers to the extent, breadth, and depth of the writing contained in the document. Scope can be broad or narrow, lim-ited or extensive, or detailed or sparse (see Exhibits 3-3 and 3-4). Defining the scope depends on readers' needs and experience levels.

EXHIBIT 3-3.   FOLLOW-UP TO DISCUSS CHARITABLE
GIFT PLANNING

This and the next letter contrast the scope of the information communicated to a donor. The first is more casual and would be sent to a donor who is experienced in charitable giving. The second provides far more detail and summarizes information previously discussed.

DOCUMENT 218

FOLLOW-UP MEETING TO DISCUSS CHARITABLE GIFT PLANNING

Dear <NAME>:

Thank you for meeting with me last week to discuss charitable gift-planning alternatives at <ORGANIZATION>. I hope the information that I provided was helpful to you. The selection of the most appropriate planning options depends on your philanthropic goals, financial objectives, and estate planning considerations.

As we discussed, I would be happy to meet with you and your wife to review the alternatives and to answer questions that you may have. Charitable gift planning takes time, so it is not unusual to see donors evaluate a series of options over a period of years to make the most appropriate choice.

If you have any questions, feel free to call me at <TELEPHONE>. Thank you.

Sincerely,

<NAME>

EXHIBIT 3-4.   FOLLOW-UP ON REQUEST FOR
INFORMATION LETTER

Note that this letter provides more extensive information and recites the benefits of the gift options. The letter reinforces information previously sent to the donor.

DOCUMENT 206

FOLLOW-UP ON REQUEST FOR INFORMATION

Dear <NAME>:

I hope you received the information I sent you last week. I wanted to follow up with you on your interest in establishing a charitable gift annuity at <ORGANIZATION>.

EXHIBIT 3-4.   FOLLOW-UP ON REQUEST FOR INFORMATION
LETTER *(Continued)*

A charitable gift annuity is a life income gift in that it provides you with an income for life, a charitable income tax deduction, and, best of all, the opportunity to designate the remainder of the annuity to the ‹NAME› Endowed Memorial Scholarship Fund.

The charitable gift annuity is based on the size of the gift and your age at the time your gift is made. For a donor age 69 who makes a $100,000 gift, the annuity rate is ‹ % ›, which provides an annual income of ‹ $ › payable monthly in the amount of ‹ $ ›. Additionally, you receive an immediate charitable income tax deduction of ‹ $ ›. The deduction is taken in the year the gift is made, or, if necessary, it can be used for up to five additional years. For a gift of cash, you may claim a charitable income tax deduction for up to 50% of your adjusted gross income.

A charitable gift annuity provides mutual benefits to both the donor and ‹ORGANIZA-TION›. As many of our donors say, "It is a win/win situation." Should you have any questions, please feel free to call at ‹TELEPHONE›. Again, thank you for considering establishing a charitable gift annuity at ‹ORGANIZATION›.

RESEARCH

To engage in planned giving and charitable gift planning and to advise others about the benefits and detriments of specific gift options requires mastery of a specific body of knowledge. To gain that knowledge, the planned giving officer must study and engage in extensive learning and research. While one must be careful when communicating verbally with an audience, one must be exceptionally precise when writing. If the document is being widely distributed or is being sent to a major donor or key nonprofit officials, this is even more true (see Exhibit 3-5).

In planned giving, it is important to reconfirm financial data, projections, calculations, and the appropriateness of the gift option for the particular needs of a donor. Is the correct asset being used to fund the gift? Is the gift option appropriate based on the donor's needs? Written documents convey a sense of authority. Donors, their professional advisors, and family members rely extensively on the information contained in these documents. The principles, concepts, and laws governing planned giving often are complicated, as are the areas of estate, financial, and tax planning that are so much a part of planned giving.

EXHIBIT 3-5.   PRESENTING PROPOSAL TO DONOR

This letter explains the benefits of a gift of stock. The writer provides detailed information about the tax consequences of the gift. The letter is based on a previous conversation between the donor and the planned giving staff member.

DOCUMENT 158

PRESENTING PROPOSAL TO DONOR EXPLAINING GIFT OF STOCK AND TAX BENEFITS

Dear ‹NAME›:

Greetings from ‹ORGANIZATION›. Following up on your earlier meeting with ‹NAME›, I am writing to present a proposal to establish the ‹DONOR NAME› Endowment for ‹DEPART-MENT/PROGRAM› at ‹ORGANIZATION›.

The endowment provides support for two of your lifelong interests at ‹ORGANIZATION›, ‹DEPARTMENT› and ‹PROGRAM›. You know very well the value of honor students to ‹ORGA-NIZATION›. These students challenge their peers to raise their academic standards and bring out the best in faculty, bringing the level of instruction to new heights. In addition, the fund provides important support to student athletes, who make major contributions to ‹ORGANIZATION› in the classroom and in sports.

You mentioned that you were interested in using ‹#› shares of ‹NAME› stock to support this endowment. Your gift of these shares would provide approximately ‹ $ › to fund the endowment at a share price of ‹ $ › per share. An endowment of $120,000 with a payout of 5% will provide $6,000 in annual income in support of this endowment. If you were to sell this stock and your cost basis was $30 a share, you would have a capital gain of $69,888 that would be taxed at 20% for a total tax of $13,977. Moreover, the estate tax on estates in excess of $1 million in 2002 to 2003 ranges from 37 to 50%; $1.5 million in 2004 to 2005 ranges from 37 to 48%; and $2 million in 2006 to 2008 ranges from 37 to 46%. Making a charitable gift of stock may provide valuable federal tax savings as follows:

1. Elimination of capital gains in the amount of $69,888 @ 20% = $13,977
2. A reduction in estate taxes $120,000 @ 37% = $44,400
3. A charitable income tax deduction of $120,000 @ 31% = $37,200

[Note: Figures are provided to illustrate benefits. Always recalculate benefits based on a current discount rate and tax laws in effect.]

Thus, your gift of stock valued at $120,000 would actually cost you much less when you consider the tax benefits. As you may know, for gifts of property such as stock, a donor may

---

EXHIBIT 3-5.   PRESENTING PROPOSAL TO DONOR *(Continued)*

---

claim charitable gifts for up to 30% of the donor's adjusted gross income. Your gift will also provide tax savings in ‹STATE› as well.

Your past support and interest in ‹ORGANIZATION› have provided educational opportunities to students, faculty, and staff and made you an important member of the ‹ORGANIZATION› community. This endowment will reaffirm your dedication and commitment to ‹ORGANIZATION› and will provide valuable financial assistance to programs of interest to you.

Should you wish, I would be happy to meet with you to answer any questions and to see whether this proposal meets your needs. Please call me at ‹TELEPHONE›. I look forward to speaking with you. Thank you for your continued interest in ‹ORGANIZATION›.

Sincerely,

‹NAME›

ORGANIZING DOCUMENTS

Well-organized documents are very helpful to readers. Documents may be organized in a variety of ways. Organization may be logical, sequential, chronological, historical, or by order of importance. To be effective, documents must be organized depending on their purpose, the information they contain, and the relationship between the writer and the reader (see Exhibit 3-6). Randomly organized documents are seldom helpful to readers. Because there is no organization, they are harder to read and write. Readers who receive poorly organized documents may infer that little thought was given to creating them.

EXHIBIT 3-6.   INFORMATION FOR FUND DESCRIPTION LETTER

This well-organized document sequentially explains information that the donor had requested. It presents the information one step at a time, making the document easy to read and follow.

DOCUMENT 196

INFORMATION FOR FUND DESCRIPTION

Dear Mr. and Mrs. ‹NAME›:

Greetings from ‹_____›! I hope you both enjoyed a nice holiday season with your family. It's always hard (although less exhausting) once the holidays are over.

EXHIBIT 3-6.   INFORMATION FOR FUND DESCRIPTION
LETTER *(Continued)*

I received some information from ‹DOCTOR NAME›, MD, who oversees our activities in pancreatic research. When I asked him about the latest developments, he shared with me that the ‹DEPARTMENT NAME› is currently engaged in a broad spectrum of research, falling into three areas: laboratory research, translational research, and clinical modalities.

In basic laboratory research, our investigators are studying the role of growth factors in promoting the growth of pancreatic cancer cells, with the hope that this research will lead to new strategies to control that growth. They are also pursuing efforts to identify a new tumor suppressor gene with data that suggest that mutations in that gene may enable the development of pancreatic cancer.

Translational research, I learned, is activities that translate basic research in the lab to application to patients. Here ‹DOCTOR NAME› is evaluating the use of new molecular workers detected in pancreatic tissue and secretions to make earlier and more precise diagnosis of pancreatic cancer.

In terms of clinical work, we are developing new endoscopy techniques to differentiate between benign and malignant lesions, while also refining techniques for eliminating lesions without surgery, using less invasive techniques.

I hope that this is helpful; I found it very interesting. You might consider directing the funds in ‹NAME› Fund to support any or all of these research efforts, or keep the funds to be used generally for pancreatic research.

At your convenience, I would be delighted to have you meet with Dr. ‹DOCTOR NAME› over lunch at the hospital, where he can tell you in greater detail about our research efforts. Or I will be visiting some other donors on the ‹DATE› and would be delighted to visit with you at your home. Please let me know your thoughts at your convenience. Best wishes.

Very truly yours,

‹NAME›

Chronological Order

Many writers organize documents in chronological order, the order in which things happened by date. Documents that record a transaction often are listed in reverse chronological order, listing first the most recent event and working backward. Donors who request a gift history may benefit from having the document organized in reverse chronological order. Documents that use chronological or reverse chronological order are usually very detailed and generally are used to record all steps, acts, or entries.

Order of Importance

Documents also may be organized based on the order of importance of the information. In most cases, the most important issue is addressed first and items of lesser importance are introduced later. Some writers prefer to list the least important issues first with the most important issue last. Regardless of the approach, consider the reader's expectations about the order of importance and determine the proper order (see Exhibit 3-7).

EXHIBIT 3-7.   AMBASSADOR PROGRAM LETTER

This document is an example of a letter organized by order of importance that is appealing, detailed, and easy to follow. The letter has been slightly edited to conserve space. It provides detailed information and clearly anticipates questions the reader is likely to ask.

DOCUMENT 230

AMBASSADOR PROGRAM

Dear ‹ESTATE AND FINANCIAL PLANNING PROFESSIONAL›:

Thank you for asking about our Planned Giving Ambassador Program. The program was designed for our alumni professionals in the estate and financial planning areas. The program's primary goal is to increase the level of gifts to ‹ORGANIZATION› by involving our alumni. They have the best opportunity to review gift planning opportunities with their clients. The secondary goal is to help our alumni professionals increase the level of interaction with their clients and provide them with support and resources to help them achieve their clients' goals and objectives.

First, some facts about ‹ORGANIZATION› Planned Giving Program:

- Active planned giving program for ‹NUMBER OF YEARS› years
- Actively manage over $‹***› million in planned gifts
- Gift opportunities include:
  - Charitable remainder trusts (annuity trusts and unitrusts)
  - Charitable lead trusts
  - Pooled income funds
  - Life estate agreements
  - Life insurance/IRA retirement plan beneficiary designations
  - Bequests from wills and living trusts
- Outside professional management
  - ‹ASSET MANAGER'S NAME› manages our planned giving portfolio

---

EXHIBIT 3-7.   AMBASSADOR PROGRAM LETTER *(Continued)*

- ◦ <NAME> provides trust administration services including checks, statements, and tax information
- <NAME> Legacy Society, consisting of donors who have included us in their estate plans (approximately < # > members)
- Encourage gifts from alumni as well as friends of <ORGANIZATION>
- Gifts can be designated to areas of donor interest
- Most important: View planned gifts as the future of our institution

We have an effective outreach to the local professional community but would like to expand and develop contacts in other geographical regions. Our intent for our Ambassador Program is to extend that reach, both into regions around the country that I can't get to within a couple of hours' drive and into our local professional community.

An Ambassador becomes our eyes and ears in the local community. We ask an Ambassador to review their account base to determine, if appropriate, one or more of their clients who would consider making a planned gift or include us in their estate plans. We also expect that you would talk about our program to your friends and associates so that the knowledge of our program increases in your local area. We would also encourage you to become active in your local alumni chapter, which would help you expand your influence in the local community. We can provide the name and address of your local alumni representative. We would also expect your help with any technical question, issue, or problem that we may not be able to resolve.

We expect Ambassadors to be knowledgeable in the estate and financial planning areas in order to best represent their clients. We also encourage Ambassadors to become certified specialists in their area of expertise: Probate, Estate Planning and Trust Law Certification for attorneys, Certified Public Accountant for accountants, Certified Financial Planner for financial planners, Certified Life Underwriter for life insurance planners, Certified Trust and Financial Advisor for trust officers, etc.

Now, what can you expect from us? The first area of support is the packet of information that is included with this letter. We leave this information with a donor during an initial visit or with a professional to educate him or her about the program. The packet includes our principal handout, "<NAME>," which explains a variety of gift opportunities. It is designed not only to answer some basic questions but also to raise additional questions that the donor can ask you or us. Also included is our <NAME> booklet, "<NAME>," which explains our legacy society; copies of our alumni newsletter, "<NAME>"; our professional newsletter, "<NAME>"; and sample booklets, which complement our "<NAME>" newsletter. We also include a campus map because some prospective donors may have never visited the campus. The map also includes a brief history of <ORGANIZATION>.

See Document 230 for the letter in its entirety.

First Draft

Once the writer has prepared, researched, and organized the subject matter of the document, one can write the first draft. First drafts should be written relatively quickly, expanding an outline (referred to in the introduction to this text) into sentences and paragraphs. Do not be overly concerned, at this point, about sentence structure, grammar, punctuation, or spelling. For the first draft simply go for quantity, thinking about your knowledge of the subject, about the reader, and about the reader's needs. Place sentences in a group to construct paragraphs, using perhaps no more than five sentences per paragraph. Make sure that paragraphs are cohesive and that each paragraph logically leads to the next.

Revision

Once the first draft is complete, it is time to revise. Reread the document and edit it or give it to a colleague to review. Make sure that the document is well organized and in context and that each sentence within a paragraph belongs in that paragraph and is in correct order. Then check to see that the paragraphs are in the proper order (see Exhibit 3-8).

When revising the letter, think about it from the reader's point of view. Does it assume too much? Too little? Is it likely to answer the reader's questions? Will the reader know what to do with the information? Is it clear what steps may be taken next?

EXHIBIT 3-8.	LETTER TO DONOR

This letter shows the benefits of revision. It provides much information in a relatively brief document and is warm and inviting.

DOCUMENT 214

LETTER TO DONOR AT END OF YEAR

Dear ‹NAME›:

Best wishes to you all at this wonderful holiday season. At this busy time of the year, we at the Office of Planned Giving would like to thank you for your continued support of ‹ORGANIZATION›. As the end of the year approaches, thoughts turn to charitable giving and the tax benefits that gifts to the ‹ORGANIZATION› can provide. You may wish to consider making a gift to benefit the ‹DEPARTMENT›.

The advantages of making a contribution at this time are significant. Charitable giving remains one of the most important means of reducing your tax burden this year. In ‹YEAR› you still can:

EXHIBIT 3-8.   LETTER TO DONOR *(Continued)*

- Make a gift by December 31, ‹YEAR› and reduce your ‹YEAR› in taxes;
- Make an outright gift to ‹ORGANIZATION› and receive a charitable tax deduction for the entire amount if you itemize your deductions;
- Make a larger gift to help qualify you to itemize your deductions;
- Donate a gift of appreciated securities and avoid capital gains taxes while still obtaining a charitable income tax deduction; and
- Make a matching gift with your employer to take full advantage of your gift.

Most important, there is the satisfaction of seeing your gift benefit ‹ORGANIZATION› that is committed to the highest standards.

An outright gift is an excellent way to give, but you may also wish to consider some strategies that make a major gift affordable through planned giving. ‹ORGANIZATION› offers numerous estate planning and planned giving options to maximize your contribution to ‹ORGANIZATION› while providing you with personal financial benefits.

The attached newsletter offers an example of a charitable gift annuity, a pooled income fund, and also a deferred gift annuity. If you would like a personal financial printout, please call us at ‹TELEPHONE›.

We are deeply grateful for your invaluable support and we hope that you will consider making a year-end gift to ‹ORGANIZATION›. We send our warmest holiday greetings and best wishes for the year ahead.

Sincerely,

‹NAME›

Enclosures:

CONCLUSION

Correspondence is one of the most effective tools that a planned giving staff member can use. Correspondence accomplishes many goals and helps to build new relationships and maintain and sustain existing ones. All correspondence should be targeted to meet the needs of the reader. Before writing, research the subject matter of the correspondence. Organize the material well, develop a quality first draft, and leave enough time for revisions. Have a colleague read complex documents to test the documents' effectiveness. Collaborative writing improves the quality of all documents.

## CHAPTER 4

Administrative Documents

INTRODUCTION

Administrative documents are the heart of a charity's planned giving program. Ideally, they are available to staff members at the inception of the program. Once a planned giving program is fully established, these documents help staff members work efficiently with an ever-growing number of donors, prospects, and internal and external constituents. Staff members that can create and access documents quickly and easily will help the program to run successfully.

This chapter discusses the administrative documents used in the planned giving process, focusing on: internal forms used to manage both donors/prospects and the nonprofit's internal constituency, such as staff and administrators, as well as the program itself; and external forms used to manage donors/prospects and outside advisors.

All members of the planned giving staff, from the director to an assistant or volunteer, use these documents. To improve efficiency, the planned giving assistant can tailor a standardized form letter to a particular donor or prospect and then have the planned giving officer involved with the donor personalize the letter. It is extremely important for the program to have one or more well-organized employees assemble, organize, maintain, and manage these documents so that they can be readily accessed and personalized.

DOCUMENTS

This chapter and the documents included in Section 4 of the CD-ROM focus exclusively on Administrative Documents. The CD-ROM contains 65 documents that perform the functions described in this chapter. In addition the following documents are specifically referenced and included in this chapter:

Document 290	Donor Intake Questionnaire
Document 284	Donor Intake Questionnaire for Real Estate

INTERNAL DOCUMENTS

Creating a successful planned giving office depends on managing various documents. Planned giving forms help a program to run smoothly and efficiently. Internal planned giving documents generally are geared toward three audiences:

1. Donors/prospects
2. Internal employees, such as other development staff members, the organization's administrators, deans, faculty, physicians, members, and volunteers
3. The planned giving office itself, to manage the program

Documents for Donors/Prospects

The heart and soul of most development programs are its donors and prospects. Correspondence sent to these individuals takes many forms. Once a prospect responds to a planned giving inquiry, staff members must begin to manage the donor/prospect internally. The planned giving officer must record and maintain an individual donor's biographical information and gift history, including the donor's date of birth, spouse's date of birth, social security number, direct deposit information for lifetime checks, and gift data (see Exhibit 4-1).

EXHIBIT 4-1.   DONOR INTAKE QUESTIONNAIRE FORM

A donor intake questionnaire can help the planned giving officer track a donor's relevant data and keep it in one place. Consider this internal form to manage a high volume of inquiries.

DOCUMENT 290

DONOR INTAKE QUESTIONNAIRE

Name _____

Spouse's Name _____

EXHIBIT 4-1.   DONOR INTAKE QUESTIONNAIRE FORM *(Continued)*

Address _____

City _____ State _____ Zip _____

Telephone (Home) _____ (Office) _____

Affiliation with Organization _____

Beneficiaries	**Age**	**Social Security Number**

Assets Used to Fund Gift

Type of Gift: _____

Type of Asset: ❏ Cash   ❏ Appreciated Securities (Stocks, Bonds, Mutual Funds)
                         ❏ Real Estate   ❏ Tangible Personal Property

Type of Real Estate: ❏ Personal Residence   ❏ Outright   ❏ Life Income Gift
                         ❏ Retained Life Estate

                         $_____ Value of Depreciable Portion

                         $_____ Value of Nondepreciable Portion

                         ❏ Farm or Ranch   ❏ Commercial Property   ❏ Vacant Land

                         Fair Market Value $_____   Cost Basis $_____

Comments _____
_____

Exhibit 4-2 presents a donor intake questionnaire that is used to manage gifts of real estate.

| EXHIBIT 4-2. | DONOR INTAKE QUESTIONNAIRE: GIFTS OF REAL ESTATE |

This form is used for donors who wish to make a gift of real estate. This document organizes all of the information related to a potential gift of real estate, such as the description of the property, title information, mortgage amount on the property, cost basis in the property, and applicable gift options.

DOCUMENT 284

DONOR INTAKE QUESTIONNAIRE

Name _____

Address _____

City _____ State _____ Zip _____

Telephone (Home) _____ (Office) _____

Description of Real Estate _____

Zoning _____

Fair Market Value $_____ Cost Basis $_____

Tax Bill Valuation $_____ Value of Land $_____ Value of Building $_____

Annual Operating Expenses $_____ Insurance $_____

Mortgage Amount $_____ Holder of Mortgage _____

Is Property Listed?   ❏ Yes   ❏ No   Length of Time on Market?_____

Type of Gift

❏ Outright Gift

❏ Retained Life Estate

    Life Income Tenants: Age:_____   Age:_____

❏ Charitable Remainder Trust

    Beneficiaries: Age:_____   Age:_____

    Comparison Rates   _____%   _____%

EXHIBIT 4-2.   DONOR INTAKE QUESTIONNAIRE:
GIFTS OF REAL ESTATE *(Continued)*

❑ Bargain Sale

Amount of Up-Front Payment $_____

Comments _____

Documents for Development Staff, Administrators, Deans, Faculty, Physicians, Members, and Volunteers

A large pool of internal staff members at the nonprofit institution helps with the planned giving process. Many of these individuals are directly involved in identifying prospects and soliciting gifts. Sometimes gifts are made in their honor, and the individual is the reason the donor is connected to the nonprofit. Working with these internal employees and keeping them involved and informed about the planned giving program and process needs to be a top priority. Documents can be used to inform internal employees that a gift has been made to benefit one of their programs or projects. Documents can be developed to sensitize nondevelopment staff about ways to identify planned giving donors and prospects (see Exhibit 4-3).

EXHIBIT 4-3.   CHECKLIST OF PROSPECTS FORM

This document is a checklist to help identify potential planned giving leads. Any staff member can periodically review the document to help build a larger prospect base.

DOCUMENT 264

CHECKLIST TO IDENTIFY MAJOR AND PLANNED GIVING PROSPECTS

Checklist to identify donors with a giving record:

❑ A donor with a solid annual giving record

❑ A loyal donor who has made gifts in three of the preceding five years

❑ Donors who have included the nonprofit organization in their wills or trust

❑ Donors who have established memorial funds or endowed funds

❑ Donors who have made outright gifts of $1,000, $5,000, or $10,000

❑ Donors who have made planned gifts

EXHIBIT 4-3.   CHECKLIST OF PROSPECTS FORM *(Continued)*

Checklist for individuals who have an established relationship with the nonprofit organization:

☐ A nondonor who appreciates her relationship with the nonprofit

☐ A volunteer or board member

☐ A family with several generations of connections with the nonprofit

☐ Faculty or staff who provide financial support to their departments through payroll deduction

☐ Staff who have been employed by the nonprofit for ten years or more

☐ Retirees or faculty emeriti

☐ Individuals who hold more than one degree from the nonprofit

☐ Donors who have attended more than three functions at the nonprofit within one year

☐ Donors who have received extended care

☐ Donors who have professional relationships with the nonprofit's staff members

Checklist to identify donors with special family considerations:

☐ A surviving spouse

☐ A couple without children

☐ A donor for whom an endowed fund is appropriate to memorialize or honor a loved one

☐ Donors who have established an endowed family fund

☐ Donors from families who have generations of involvement with the nonprofit

Checklist for financial savvy donors:

☐ A professional advisor

☐ A donor with JD, Ph.D., MD, DDS, CPA, CFP in her title

☐ A person familiar with investments and financial statements

☐ Graduates of professional schools

☐ Employees of financial institutions

☐ An entrepreneur or chief executive officer

☐ Donors with large holdings of investment assets such as real estate, stocks, bonds, or mutual funds

☐ A donor interested in supplementing retirement earnings

☐ Attendees of a nonprofit organization's retirement planning workshop

☐ Donors seeking to stabilize income during retirement

☐ Individuals holding traditionally lower paying professional positions who were long-term employees

☐ Donors seeking to provide benefits for spouses

Planned Giving Program

Running a planned giving program requires lots of focused internal administration. An office can create various documents to remind staff members of the next steps to be taken in tracking or monitoring prospects or donors. Documents also can be developed to help plan events and programs.

Hiring staff is one of the most important parts of a planned giving program (see Exhibit 4-4). The appendix and accompanying CD-ROM contain a number of other documents that can assist in recruiting qualified staff.

EXHIBIT 4-4.   PLANNED GIVING JOB DESCRIPTION

This document is used to attract qualified candidates to serve as the nonprofit's planned giving officer. The ad can be modified easily to meet the specific needs of the employer.

DOCUMENT 243

PLANNED GIVING OFFICER JOB DESCRIPTION

Announcement of Position Availability

Title:	Planned Giving Officer
Employer:	Reports to ‹TITLE›
Effective Date:	‹DATE›
Salary:	Competitive Salary

Qualifications:

- Bachelor's degree required, advanced degree preferred.
- A minimum of 5 years experience in a major nonprofit organization.
- Candidate must demonstrate the following skills and abilities:
  1. Success in soliciting significant planned gifts
  2. The ability to forge strong working relationships with others and have a capacity for engendering confidence and trust
  3. Exceptional interpersonal and communication skills
  4. High motivation level and consistent follow-through
  5. Technical proficiency

Responsibilities:

- Cultivate and solicit planned gifts (‹ $ › and up).

EXHIBIT 4-4.   PLANNED GIVING JOB DESCRIPTION *(Continued)*

- Train ‹ORGANIZATION›'s staff, boards, and volunteers in planned giving options and use of various assets.
- Initiate a marketing program for planned giving.
- Assist ‹ORGANIZATION›'s development staff in identifying, cultivating, and soliciting planned giving prospects.
- Provide technical support and planned giving expertise to professional advisors.
- Implement and manage planned giving program and manage staff.

Benefits Offered: ‹LIST BENEFITS›.

Deadline for Applications: Submit cover letter and resume by ‹DATE›.

Apply to: ‹NAME, TITLE›
‹ORGANIZATION›
‹ADDRESS›
‹CITY, STATE ZIP›

Another useful document for any office is a statement of program goals (see Exhibit 4-5). If the planned giving office is new, use this document to keep the staff on track to build a planned giving program in year 1.

EXHIBIT 4-5.   PLANNED GIVING GOALS

This document establishes achievable goals and can be distributed to planned giving office staff members. Assignments can be delegated to individual staff members.

DOCUMENT 253

PLANNED GIVING GOALS

Specific Goals for Year One

☐   Learn planned giving basics through education.

☐   Build up a planned giving network of colleagues who can provide support and advice.

☐   Select outside assistance, such as an attorney and a planned giving consultant.

☐   Create a management plan for one year.

☐   Decide whether to create a pooled income fund and/or to offer charitable gift annuities.

EXHIBIT 4-5.   PLANNED GIVING GOALS *(Continued)*

❏ Identify the most effective and realistic marketing tools. Use as many of the following options as possible:

- Advertisements in existing publications

- A planned giving check-off box on annual fund appeals

- A targeted mail piece to planned giving prospects

- A planned giving brochure to illustrate benefits

- Sample bequest language for donors and attorneys

- An existing event at the organization to promote planned giving

❏ Select several planned giving prospects from the donor base to begin to solicit for a planned gift.

❏ Work with the treasurer's office to define gift administration and/or select an outside manager to administer pooled income fund gifts and charitable gift annuities.

❏ Select a software package, especially if the organization establishes a pooled income fund and offers charitable gift annuities.

❏ Determine the parameters for crediting gifts.

EXTERNAL FORMS

Planned giving administrative documents also must be managed and organized for the program's external audience. These forms are correspondence sent outside the office or institution to donors/prospects and to a program's outside advisors.

Prospects and Donors

Prospects and donors receive many types of correspondence from the planned giving office, including marketing efforts, solicitation letters, standard planned giving letters with calculations, and standardized forms such as applications to make different life income gifts, pledge forms, instructions to make a gift of securities, and bequest commitments. The planned giving membership application invites donors to indicate whether they have made a planned gift to a charity (see Exhibit 4-6).

EXHIBIT 4-6.   GIVING SOCIETY MEMBERSHIP APPLICATION FORM

The Planned Giving Society Membership Application is distributed to donors and prospects who have or may have made a qualifying planned gift to the nonprofit. Donors complete and return these forms. Often the charity first learns about a planned gift when a donor returns this form to the nonprofit.

EXHIBIT 4-6.   GIVING SOCIETY MEMBERSHIP APPLICATION
FORM *(Continued)*

DOCUMENT 294

GIVING SOCIETY MEMBERSHIP APPLICATION

‹PLANNED GIVING SOCIETY› Membership Application

Name _____

Mailing Address _____

‹COLLEGE/IF ALUMNUS OR ALUMNA› _____

Relationship to ‹ORGANIZATION› (if non-alumnus or -alumna) _____

Type of Provision

I have made a provision for ‹ORGANIZATION› in my estate.

Estimated Amount

plan as follows:

1. Outright bequest in will:

    (a)   Specific dollar amount $_____

    (b)   Specific property (please describe) $_____

    _____

    (c)   Share of entire residue of estate (_____ %) $_____

2. Conditional bequest or will (please describe conditions) $_____

    _____

3. Trust under will or to be funded by will (please describe)

    (a)   Charitable Remainder Trust $_____

    _____

    (b)   Charitable Lead Trust $_____

    _____

    (c)   Other $_____

    _____

4. As beneficiary of a life insurance policy $_____

    _____

EXHIBIT 4-6.   GIVING SOCIETY MEMBERSHIP APPLICATION
FORM *(Continued)*

5.   Other (please describe) $_____

_____

If your gift to ‹ORGANIZATION› is for other than ‹ORGANIZATION›'s general purposes, please describe any restrictions on the back of this form. Attachments or letters that further describe the above provision(s) are encouraged. In particular, a copy of the section of your will, trust agreement, or other document containing the provision(s) will be appreciated. In the event of unforeseen circumstances that require any further change in the above estate planning provision(s), I agree to notify ‹ORGANIZATION› of such change.

_____   _____
Date   Signature

Please return this form to: ‹NAME›, ‹TITLE›, ‹ADDRESS, CITY, STATE ZIP›; ‹TELEPHONE›.

A second external form sent to a prospect is an application form to create a charitable gift annuity (see Exhibit 4-7). This form compiles and manages information about the donor's gift.

EXHIBIT 4-7.   GIFT ANNUITY APPLICATION FORM

This form provides the planned giving office with all of the information required to move ahead with finalizing the donor's charitable gift annuity. It includes such information as the names of the life income beneficiaries from the gift, a description of the asset used to make the gift, and where to send the donor's gift annuity checks.

DOCUMENT 289

GIFT ANNUITY APPLICATION

Name _____

Address _____

Telephone _____

Date of Birth _____

EXHIBIT 4-7. GIFT ANNUITY APPLICATION FORM *(Continued)*

Name(s) of person(s), birth date, and social security # to whom annuity is to be paid:

_____

If the annuity is to be paid to two persons:

❏ Should the annuity check be made payable to
   both persons while both are living?

❏ Should the checks be made payable to one person
   for life then to other person for life?

If the annuity checks are to be made payable to one person for life and then to the other person for life, who is to receive the annuity first: _____

If the annuity will be established with cash, amount of cash to be used: _____

If the annuity will be established with marketable securities, description of securities:

Owner of securities: _____

Approximate current value: _____

Cost basis of securities: _____

How long were securities held? _____

When do you want annuity payments to begin?

❏ Immediately (as opposed to deferred for one or more years)

❏ In _____ years

Where do you want annuity checks sent?

Name: _____

Address: _____

_____

May we use your name in future publications?

❏ Yes   ❏ No

Signature: _____

Advisors

External planned giving documents also include correspondence to an outside advisor who interacts with the planned giving program and can act as a source to the program for new donors and prospects (see Exhibit 4-8). An outside advisor may be currently counseling a client who is a donor or could become a donor in the future. Build relationships with existing and new advisors through marketing efforts such as periodic outreach letters, year-end thank-you letters, and general correspondence about the organization. Distribute the nonprofit's gift acceptance policy to all advisors. Often a discussion and explanation of the policy generates inquiries by advisors on behalf of clients who hold specific assets addressed in the policy.

EXHIBIT 4-8.   GIFT ACCEPTANCE POLICY

This is an excerpt from a sample gift acceptance policy included on the CD-ROM. To view the rest of this document, see Document 260.

DOCUMENT 260

SAMPLE GIFT ACCEPTANCE POLICY #2

Introduction

Purpose: This gift policy is intended to guide the staff at ‹ORGANIZATION› (‹ORGANIZATION›) and its affiliates when discussing current and deferred gifts with individual donors, their advisors, and organizations. It is intended to establish processes to accept these types of gifts and administer them at ‹ORGANIZATION›.

Status: ‹ORGANIZATION› is a tax-exempt organization as defined in Section 501(c)(3) of the Internal Revenue Code of 1986. The federal tax identification number for ‹ORGANIZATION› is ‹#›.

Approved: These policies were last approved ‹DATE›.

I.   GIFT ADMINISTRATION—GENERAL

    A.   Gift Processing

        1.   Coordination among All Offices

‹ORGANIZATION› recognizes that accurately processing a gift in a timely manner is complex and important to both the donor and the ‹ORGANIZATION›. Therefore, all efforts will be made to coordinate the process among the Development Office, the Treasurer's Office, the General Accounting Office, the Medical Service Business Office, the Office of the General Counsel, and the Real Estate Office. In addition, anyone else who should know about the gift, such as the president, a physician, or a trustee, also should be notified in a timely fashion so that a

---

EXHIBIT 4-8. GIFT ACCEPTANCE POLICY *(Continued)*

---

letter of thanks can be sent from the appropriate party to the donor. The Development Office will assume primary responsibility to ensure the gift process is correct and thorough.

2. Providing Gift Receipts

‹ORGANIZATION› provides a gift receipt in accordance with IRS guidelines. This means that the donor will be informed of any quid pro quo arrangements in the gift transaction or lack thereof. In late 1996, the IRS issued final regulations that:

- Determine whether and how much of a charitable contribution is deductible;
- Provide instructions on how to substantiate gifts of $250 or more;
- Provide disclosure requirements for quid pro quo contributions over $75.

Accordingly, ‹ORGANIZATION› will rely on these regulations to advise donors on their deductions.

For deferred gifts, ‹ORGANIZATION› provides calculations that show the value of the asset donated and the remainder value (i.e., the donor's charitable income tax deduction). In addition, a computation showing how the remainder value was calculated will be provided to the donor by ‹ORGANIZATION›.

B. Non-Cash Gift Assets

1. Real Estate

‹ORGANIZATION› requires a Level 1 environmental audit to be conducted for all proposed gifts of nonresidential real estate. While this is expected to be an expense of the donor, an environmental audit—unlike a qualified appraisal—benefits ‹ORGANIZATION› in its decision to accept or reject the asset; thus ‹ORGANIZATION› may be prepared to pay for the environmental audit provided that other conditions of acceptance are approved.

Representatives from the Development and Real Estate Offices will conduct a personal inspection of all real estate, including residential real estate, proposed as a gift. A gift of real estate will not be accepted unless the inspection is satisfactory.

2. Bargain Sale Agreements—Securities

The ‹ORGANIZATION› Treasurer's Office works closely with executives from ‹FINANCIAL MANAGER› to structure gifts of securities made as bargain sales. ‹ORGANIZATION› purchases the donor's securities at an amount lower than the market value. The difference between the market value of the securities and the amount ‹ORGANIZATION› pays for the securities results in the donor's gift to ‹ORGANIZATION›. If the transaction takes time to close and if the ultimate value of the securities is unknown at the time of the gift, the gift will be booked as a pledge.

Example:

$100,000	Market value of securities
$ 85,000	‹ORGANIZATION› purchase price for securities
$ 15,000	Amount of donor's gift

EXHIBIT 4-8.   GIFT ACCEPTANCE POLICY *(Continued)*

Before the transaction is begun, a representative from ‹FINANCIAL MANAGER› works with the ‹ORGANIZATION› Treasurer's Office to discuss the discount rate that will be used for the transaction. Preferably this is 15%, but lower rates will be considered depending on the size of the gift and ‹ORGANIZATION›'s relationship with the donor.

It is expected that ‹ORGANIZATION› may engage in developing bargain sale arrangements with other privately held companies that are closely associated with supporting ‹ORGANIZATION›'s mission.

3. Other Types of Non-Cash Gift Assets

Other types of gift assets also may be acceptable to the ‹ORGANIZATION›. They include gifts of tangible personal property, oil and gas interests, partnership interests, family limited partnerships, and other assets.

C. Appraisals

Generally, if a donor intends to claim a deduction of more than $5,000 for a non-cash gift either outright or in trust, the IRS requires the donor to obtain a qualified appraisal and report a summary of that appraisal on IRS Form 8283. Exceptions to this general rule are: (1) if the gift consists of publicly traded securities, no appraisal is required; and (2) if the gift consists of closely held stock, an appraisal is required for gifts exceeding $10,000. An authorized individual in the ‹ORGANIZATION› Treasurer's Office will acknowledge the appraisal summary on Form 8283. ‹ORGANIZATION› keeps a copy of the signed appraisal in its files.

The ‹ORGANIZATION› Development Office reserves the right to obtain and pay for an additional appraisal if it determines that it is prudent to do so.

The ‹ORGANIZATION› Development Office must inform donors that if a non-cash gift for which the donor was required to file the Form 8283 is sold within two years of the date of gift, ‹ORGANIZATION›, as required by law, will complete and submit IRS Form 8282.

Generally, unless special circumstances exist, the ‹ORGANIZATION› Development Office will use its best efforts to sell a non-cash gift as soon as possible and at the highest value available.

D. Legal and Tax Counsel

The donor should have legal counsel representing him or her in most planned and outright gift transactions. Legal counsel should review and approve the language of any document and the viability of the planned gift design within the context of the donor's financial and estate plans.

If the donor wishes to receive a recommendation for legal counsel, the ‹ORGANIZATION› Development Office can provide the donor with suggested names.

Conclusion

Creating, using, managing, and maintaining administrative documents for a planned giving program can make the difference between a program staying at its current level and moving to the next level and growing its success.

Focus on forms that are used internally for donors/prospects, staff, and the program itself and those that are used externally for donors/prospects and outside advisors. Empower one or more planned giving staff members to prepare forms, and appoint one well-organized member of the staff to keep these documents organized and accessible.

## CHAPTER 5

Exhibits

INTRODUCTION

Exhibits, which classify information using visual forms of expression to communicate, include charts, graphs, tables, training materials, estate planning documents, and other documents. Exhibits are powerful communication tools that can make complex concepts easily understood. This chapter explores the ways exhibits can be designed and used to present information to a variety of audiences including donors, prospects, staff members, professional advisors, and others.

DOCUMENTS

This chapter and the documents included in Section 5 of the CD-ROM focus exclusively on Exhibits. The CD-ROM contains 28 documents that perform the functions described in this chapter. In addition the following documents are specifically referenced and included in this chapter:

Document 319	Estate Tax Chart
Document 307	Planned Giving Training Quiz
Document 309	The Capital Campaign
Document 310	Development Plan for Nondevelopment Staff
Document 332	Sample Bequest Language
Document 321	Personal Budget and Net Worth Statement

PURPOSES

Exhibits are used for a variety of purposes, including:

- Presenting technical information
- Comparing advantages or disadvantages of two or more alternatives
- Demonstrating increases or decreases in two or more alternatives

- Presenting data that is based on numbers, quantities, or amounts
- Communicating information
- Presenting complex information with less repetition

TYPES OF EXHIBITS

A variety of exhibits can be used to present data and numerical information. The following sections offer an overview.

Graphs

Graphs contrast and compare numerical data and show trends. Most graphs are oriented on two axes. Often one axis shows a numerical scale and the other axis shows time.

Tables

Tables typically are organized into rows and columns. The rows and columns may each have headings, or just one or the other may. A table usually shows considerable information and focuses on particular subject matter (see Exhibit 5-1).

EXHIBIT 5-1.   ESTATE AND GIFT TAX RATES AND CREDIT EXEMPTIONS

This table shows information about the estate and gift tax rates and the amounts that can be exempted from taxation over a period of years. The headings, rows, and columns organize the information.

DOCUMENT 319

ESTATE TAX CHART

Calendar Year	Estate and GST Tax Deathtime Transfer Exemption	Gift Transfer Exemption Tax	Highest Estate and Gift Tax Rates
2002	$1 million	$1 million	50%
2003	$1 million	$1 million	49%
2004	$1.5 million	$1 million	48%
2005	$1.5 million	$1 million	47%
2006	$2 million	$1 million	46%
2007	$2 million	$1 million	45%
2008	$2 million	$1 million	45%
2009	$3.5 million	$1 million	45%
2010	N/A (taxes repealed)	$1 million	Maximum gift tax rate equal to maximum income tax rate (35%)

Charts

Charts compare and contrast data and illustrate trends over periods of time. Types of charts include:

- *Bar charts.* Bar charts often compare the number of units along a scale compared to units measured in other years.
- *Line charts.* Line charts compare items over time to show a direction and a correlation, such as showing how charitable gift annuity rates increase with age.
- *Pie charts.* Pie charts show parts of a whole. For example, one pie chart could show the most common types of investment assets used by donors. While pie charts are based on 100% of something, they may be based on time, such as 24 hours.

Training Materials

Training materials include a variety of documents that can be used as teaching materials during seminars, workshops, or lectures. Training materials include:

- Planned giving training program
- Planned giving quiz
- Agenda for financial planning workshop
- Overview of a capital campaign
- Development plan

Each document is designed to inform the audience about a particular topic. Some of these documents are designed to be interactive, inviting the audience to participate in the process (see Exhibits 5-2, 5-3, and 5-4).

EXHIBIT 5-2.   PLANNED GIVING TRAINING QUIZ SAMPLE

This quiz draws the audience into the subject matter of planned giving. It is used to test the audience's knowledge of the subject matter after attending a training session.

DOCUMENT 307

PLANNED GIVING TRAINING QUIZ

Please circle the correct True or False answer.

1. Many planned gift options provide a donor with an income for life.   T   F

EXHIBIT 5-2.   PLANNED GIVING TRAINING QUIZ SAMPLE *(Continued)*

2. By funding a charitable gift annuity with appreciated securities,   T   F
    a donor can avoid paying tax on the capital gain of the gifted asset.

3. Donors can make a gift of real estate to ‹ORGANIZATION› and live in   T   F
    their home for their lifetime.

4. When making a gift through a deferred gift annuity, a donor takes her   T   F
    charitable tax deduction in the year she begins receiving an income.

5. The greatest amount of money received by nonprofits is from charitable   T   F
    bequests.

6. A charitable remainder annuity trust pays a donor a variable rate of   T   F
    return based on the amount of the trust's principal revalued annually.

7. A pooled income fund provides a donor with a fixed income either for   T   F
    a term of years or for life.

8. The capital gains tax is currently at a maximum rate of 20%.   T   F

9. Planned gifts are a substitute for cash gifts.   T   F

10. There is a planned giving option available that allows a donor to make   T   F
    a gift to ‹ORGANIZATION› without using any current assets.

EXHIBIT 5-3.   OVERVIEW OF A CAPITAL CAMPAIGN

This overview of a capital campaign can be used with a variety of groups.
It educates individuals about the reasons for a campaign and defines the
purposes of a campaign.

DOCUMENT 309

THE CAPITAL CAMPAIGN

Overview of a Campaign for ‹ORGANIZATION›

A campaign:

- Supplements traditional financial resources.
- Unifies ‹ORGANIZATION›.
- Provides organization and structure.
- Provides a focus on ‹ORGANIZATION›, its people, programs, and mission.
- Invigorates internal and external ‹ORGANIZATION› constituents.

EXHIBIT 5-3.   OVERVIEW OF A CAPITAL CAMPAIGN *(Continued)*

- Identifies new volunteer leadership.
- Attracts new donors.
- Strengthens ‹ORGANIZATION› programs.
- Builds ‹ORGANIZATION› partnerships.
- Builds regional, national, and international networks.

A campaign does not:

- Offset budget deficits.
- Fund all ‹ORGANIZATION› needs.
- Fund all identified campaign goals.
- Succeed without the support of all ‹ORGANIZATION› personnel.

EXHIBIT 5-4.   DEVELOPMENT PLAN

This development plan for nondevelopment staff at an educational institution is used as a worksheet with nonprofit individuals and groups including development staff, deans, directors, department heads, faculty, staff, volunteers, and board members. This plan also demonstrates the role of the nondevelopment staff. This exhibit is designed to make the reader consider ways to build a development and planned giving program. The document can be used one-on-one or with groups.

DOCUMENT 310

DEVELOPMENT PLAN FOR NONDEVELOPMENT STAFF

Major Constituents

A department's major constituents are known by key representatives within the department. A brainstorming session can help identify potential sources of support. Constituents come from the following groups:

- Educational institutions: alumni
- Hospitals: patients
- Arts/cultural organizations: patrons
- Friends
- Past and present donors

EXHIBIT 5-4.   DEVELOPMENT PLAN *(Continued)*

- Past and present faculty and staff
- Vendors with whom the department does business or purchases products/services
- Parents or family members of key persons in the department
- Employers or industries that hire the department's employees/products
- Entities that depend on the department for research or technical support
- Past and present board members or advisory committees
- Those who attend or participate in the department's programs, services, or activities

Key Issues

To focus the development effort, the following 10 questions must be answered:

1. What are the department's needs?
2. Who are its constituents?
3. Which of the department's employees have valuable relationships with constituents?
4. Who, on behalf of the department, needs to be involved in working with the prospect?
5. Are there working committees and volunteers that can be mobilized?
6. Is there agreement on priorities and objectives?
7. Which types of gifts are appropriate to meet the needs?
8. Which type of solicitation is the most appropriate for the prospect?
9. Can the effort be sustained over time?
10. Is the entire department behind the effort?

Development Initiatives

The following 21 development initiatives can be implemented to assist the department in its fund-raising efforts:

1. Identify new prospects and cultivate existing donors.
2. Identify and work with volunteers who are willing to solicit others for a major gift.
3. Segment the database to develop a targeted population of donors who have made annual gifts of $100 or more for three or more years.
4. Segment the database to select donors or prospects who are 70 years or older to send specific development information, such as information on life income gifts and bequests.

EXHIBIT 5-4.   DEVELOPMENT PLAN *(Continued)*

---

5. Send a letter from the department head to all donors who have given $5,000 or more cumulatively.

6. Target geographical areas for a focused visibility effort.

7. Create advertisements and articles for existing newsletters or publications.

8. Offer a planned giving, financial planning, or estate planning column in a newsletter.

9. Identify and publicize funding opportunities and needs through various publications.

10. At year-end, send donors and prospects a year-end tax letter that highlights the benefits of charitable giving and current tax incentives.

11. Mail a "Ways to Give" brochure to retired faculty, staff, and administrators along with a letter showing the benefits of making gifts.

12. To outline the department's mission, host a series of events for donors, prospects, and friends of the organization who may be capable of making a major gift.

13. Host a luncheon for all donors who have made major gifts to the organization.

14. Conduct screening meetings with volunteers, staff, and donors to identify new prospects.

15. Host a series of breakfast meetings for specific geographical regions.

16. Meet with staff to make them aware of fund-raising needs. Meet with them in small groups or individually to discuss prospects. Distribute funding opportunities.

17. Devote the next issue of a newsletter to the development program. Overprint to have the document serve as additional solicitation literature. State goals, objectives, needs, fund-raising opportunities.

18. Establish quarterly and yearly timetables, develop an action plan, establish goals, and assign responsibilities.

19. Guest lectures/symposiums: Recognize that those who attend events, programs, or activities are likely to be good prospects.

20. Focus on the process of identifying, cultivating, and soliciting prospects and donors.

21. Follow up with all attendees for every activity, event, or program.

Implementation

- Participate in the Annual Giving Program.
- Consult with the Office of Development for ways to include planned giving in your Development Program.
- Organize staff in the field to meet with donors/prospects.
- Draft model proposals and letters to individuals.

EXHIBIT 5-4.   DEVELOPMENT PLAN *(Continued)*

- Establish a Friends Program.
- Identify a Top 100 list of prospects/donors.
- Assign prospects/donors through prospect management to the appropriate college staff.
- Place articles in magazines or newspapers.
- Identify, cultivate, and solicit 20 to 25 prospects.
- Follow up.

Estate Planning Documents

Estate planning documents can be used to illustrate estate planning concepts. The ones presented here can serve as model documents. The documents include:

- Will
- Revocable living trust
- Durable power of attorney
- Personal information record
- Healthcare proxy
- Net worth statement and budget
- Long-term healthcare worksheet
- Long-term healthcare fact sheet
- Sample bequest language
- Other documents on settling and probating an estate

These exhibits show visually the documents that are needed to develop an estate plan and settle an estate. The documents are helpful to nonprofit staff members, donors, prospects, and volunteers. Because many people do not have a will, many donors, staff members, and volunteers are unfamiliar with the physical appearance of this document and with its language and clauses. Development staff members and volunteers are not likely to be comfortable talking to donors and prospects about something that is foreign to them. These documents encourage individuals to consider their own estate planning needs and make it easier for staff members to discuss estate planning with donors and prospects. For example, during an estate planning seminar, it is helpful to show a simple will to illustrate ways donors can make gifts through a bequest. The CD-ROM contains a will, trust, sample bequest language, along with many other related documents (see Exhibits 5-5 and 5-6).

EXHIBIT 5-5.   SAMPLE BEQUEST LANGUAGE DOCUMENT

This document serves as a model for individuals interested in making distributions from their estates to a nonprofit organization. The exhibit can be produced as a separate document or can be included in a variety of development publications.

DOCUMENT 332

SAMPLE BEQUEST LANGUAGE

Bequests to ‹ORGANIZATION›

A bequest to ‹ORGANIZATION› is a way of perpetuating a donor's support for the role ‹ORGANIZATION› plays in the lives of others. It also enables a donor to make a major gift that might not otherwise be possible.

Through a bequest a donor may leave to ‹ORGANIZATION› a specific dollar amount, for example, ($10,000), or may reserve for ‹ORGANIZATION› all or a certain percentage of the estate after provisions for family members and other beneficiaries have been made. The donor may stipulate whether the bequest is for the general support of ‹ORGANIZATION› or for a specific purpose. A bequest may also be made in honor or memory of another individual.

In addition to cash and securities, bequests to ‹ORGANIZATION› may include real estate, works of art, or patent rights. All outright bequests to ‹ORGANIZATION› are exempt from federal estate taxes, and there is no limitation on the size of the gift.

Suggested Forms of Bequests

When making or revising a will, a donor should obtain the assistance of an attorney. Members of ‹ORGANIZATION›'s Office of Development will be pleased to work with you and your attorney to design an estate plan specifically tailored to your wishes. The following are suggested forms for making various types of bequests.

1. Outright bequest in will

    (a) Specific dollar amount:

    "I bequeath the sum of $＿＿＿＿＿ to ‹ORGANIZATION›, ‹CITY, STATE ZIP›, to be used or disposed of as its Board of Directors in its sole discretion deems appropriate."

    (b) Specific property (personal property):

    "I bequeath ‹DESCRIPTION OF PROPERTY› to ‹ORGANIZATION›, ‹CITY, STATE ZIP›, to be used or disposed of as its Board of Directors in its sole discretion deems appropriate."

EXHIBIT 5-5.   SAMPLE BEQUEST LANGUAGE DOCUMENT *(Continued)*

    (c)   Specific property (real estate):

"I devise all of my right, title, and interest in and to the real estate located at ‹DESCRIPTION OF PROPERTY› to ‹ORGANIZATION›, ‹CITY, STATE ZIP›, to be used or disposed of as its Board of Directors in its sole discretion deems appropriate."

    (d)   Share, or entire residue, of estate:

"I devise and bequeath (all/or _____ %) of the remainder of my property to ‹ORGANIZATION›, ‹CITY, STATE ZIP›, to be used or disposed of as its Board of Directors in its sole discretion deems appropriate."

2. **Conditional bequest in will**

Insert the conditional language in one or more of the above provisions. For example:

"If my husband/wife does not survive me, I bequeath the sum of $_____ to the ‹ORGANIZATION›, ‹CITY, STATE ZIP›, to be used or disposed of as its Board of Directors in its sole discretion deems appropriate."

If the gift to ‹ORGANIZATION› is for a purpose other than ‹ORGANIZATION›'s unrestricted use, insert the restriction in place of the words "to be used or disposed of as its Board of Directors in its sole discretion deems appropriate." For example:

"I bequeath the sum of $_____ to ‹ORGANIZATION›, ‹CITY, STATE ZIP›, for the following use and purpose: ‹DESCRIPTION OF PURPOSE›." In the event of a gift subject to a restriction, we suggest including one of the following provisions:

"However, I impose no legal or equitable obligation in this regard."

or

"If in the judgment of the Board of Directors of ‹ORGANIZATION›, it becomes impossible to accomplish the purposes of this gift, the income or principal may be used for such related purposes and in such manner as determined by its Board of Directors."

For further information please contact: ‹NAME›
    ‹ORGANIZATION›
    ‹TITLE›
    ‹ADDRESS›
    ‹CITY, STATE ZIP›
    ‹TELEPHONE›

EXHIBIT 5-6.   PERSONAL BUDGET AND NET WORTH STATEMENT

Documents like this exhibit help individuals consider the nature and extent of their resources that may be used to make gifts to charity.

DOCUMENT 321

PERSONAL BUDGET AND NET WORTH STATEMENT

Income	Self	Spouse
Salary	$_____	$_____
Bonus	$_____	$_____
Other Compensation	$_____	$_____
Dividends	$_____	$_____
Interest Income	$_____	$_____
Rent	$_____	$_____
Royalties	$_____	$_____
Business Profits	$_____	$_____
Trust Income	$_____	$_____
Capital Gain Income	$_____	$_____
Tax-Free Income	$_____	$_____
Total Income	$_____	

Expenses	Self	Spouse
Food	$_____	$_____
Clothing	$_____	$_____
Housing	$_____	$_____
Maintenance	$_____	$_____

EXHIBIT 5-6.   PERSONAL BUDGET AND NET WORTH
STATEMENT *(Continued)*

Utilities	$ _____	$ _____
Telephone	$ _____	$ _____
Property Taxes	$ _____	$ _____
State Taxes	$ _____	$ _____
Federal Taxes	$ _____	$ _____
Social Security	$ _____	$ _____
Sales Taxes	$ _____	$ _____
Medical	$ _____	$ _____
Dental	$ _____	$ _____
Prescriptions	$ _____	$ _____
Education	$ _____	$ _____
Personal Care	$ _____	$ _____
Child Care	$ _____	$ _____
Travel	$ _____	$ _____
Entertainment	$ _____	$ _____
Life Insurance	$ _____	$ _____
Auto Insurance	$ _____	$ _____
Property Insurance	$ _____	$ _____
Medical Insurance	$ _____	$ _____
Debt Reduction	$ _____	$ _____
Savings	$ _____	$ _____
Investments	$ _____	$ _____
Total Expenses	$ _____	

EXHIBIT 5-6.   PERSONAL BUDGET AND NET WORTH
STATEMENT *(Continued)*

NET WORTH STATEMENT

Assets	FMV	Liabilities	FMV
Savings	$_____	Accounts Payable	$_____
Checking	$_____	Loans	$_____
CDs	$_____	Mortgages	$_____
Money Market	$_____	Taxes Owed	$_____
Notes	$_____	Credit Card Debt	$_____
Receivables	$_____	Total Liabilities/FMV	$_____
Stocks	$_____	Total Assets	$_____
Bonds	$_____	(Total Liabilities)	$_____
Mutual Funds	$_____	**Net Worth** (assets less liabilities)	$_____
Retirement Benefits	$_____		
Personal Property	$_____		
Antiques	$_____		
Real Estate	$_____		
Automobiles	$_____		
Life Insurance	$_____		
Business Interests	$_____		
Collectibles	$_____		
Patents	$_____		
Trademarks	$_____		
Copyrights	$_____		
Total Assets/FMV	$_____		

Agendas

Like most agendas, the financial planning agenda is designed to organize a seminar and give the audience an overview of the type of information to be presented. The agenda orients and places in context the subject matter of the workshop.

USING EXHIBITS

When using exhibits, be sure to consider the audience. Each exhibit should contain:

- A descriptive title
- Legends or labels
- Points of orientation for the reader

Always take time to explain to the audience the type of information that is contained in the exhibit and how the exhibit relates to the general subject matter. If the exhibit contains technical information, make sure it has a legend or other descriptor to help the audience better understand the information. Never refer to an exhibit without providing an explanation and never assume that the audience will understand an exhibit on its face.

Some individuals respond better to verbal communications while others appreciate visual communications, such as exhibits, to help clarify or present information. People who are employed in the sciences, business, finance, mathematics, engineering, and related occupations are used to seeing technical charts and graphs. Other audiences may be less familiar with them. Consider the education and expertise level of the audience before selecting a particular method of presenting the information.

TROUBLESHOOTING

Before using exhibits, anticipate potential problems that could interfere with the planned giving staff member who is making the presentation or with the audience in understanding the information presented. Troubleshoot the exhibits to increase staff members' confidence and the usefulness of the exhibits. Before using exhibits, ask:

- Has the research been confirmed? An exhibit is only as good as the research on which it is based.
- Does the exhibit reinforce the verbal message?
- Has the appropriate type of exhibit been selected?
- Is the exhibit properly formatted?
- Is the exhibit too complex or too busy?

CONCLUSION

Exhibits are working documents that accomplish much on behalf of planned giving staff members, individuals, groups, and other audiences. These documents illustrate complex concepts and promote action. They tend to break down barriers and involve individuals and groups in the subject matter. Exhibits are hands-on tools that motivate and engage audiences.

## CHAPTER 6

Planned Giving Presentations

INTRODUCTION

Planned giving presentations are an increasingly important component of a planned giving officer's job responsibilities. A presentation on planned giving provides an opportunity to introduce important technical and practical information about planned giving options and the use of various assets and communicates the nonprofit's message to its internal and external constituents. A presentation can be made to donors, prospects, friends, staff, volunteers, board members, and professional advisors.

Presentations to donors and friends, and in the case of colleges and universities to alumni groups, serve as social gatherings for cultivation and reacquaintance with representatives from the nonprofit that can strengthen the donor's bond with the nonprofit and lead to increased financial support. Presentations to staff members, nonprofit officials, and development staff members create opportunities for these groups to learn about planned giving. Presentations to volunteers and board members are usually for training purposes in the hope that the audience will use the information for personal planning or in their fund-raising capacity to solicit planned gifts. Presentations to professional advisors are part of the nonprofit's public education and outreach program to educate listeners about its needs and charitable gift planning options that are available.

A thoughtful and purposeful planned giving presentation is also a solicitation of the attendees. In order not to lose this important opportunity, make sure the presentation is of the highest quality. Sophisticated audiences are accustomed to seeing savvy financial planners and investment brokers offer state-of-the-art presentations that use color, graphics, and audio-visual materials to communicate potentially complicated information. A high-quality presentation requires careful preparation and effective visual forms of communication such as slides, overheads, transparencies, and PowerPoint presentations.

This chapter explores the issues associated with planned giving presentations and offers a master set of documents, which may be used or modified to meet the needs of the planned giving officer and the audience.

Documents

This chapter and the documents included in Section 6 of the CD-ROM focus exclusively on Presentations. The CD-ROM contains 40 documents that perform the functions described in this chapter. The master set of documents is divided into six sections:

1. Introduction to planned giving
2. Life income gifts
3. Tax consequences of charitable gifts
4. Estate planning—wills and trusts
5. Asset classification
6. Building endowments

The master set of documents, called Master Presentation Inventory, is included at the end of this chapter (see Exhibit 6-1). It is provided in its entirety to give readers a better sense of these documents. In compiling individual presentations, select those exhibits or parts of the exhibit that are most relevant to the intended audience; not all of the exhibits will be used in a single presentation. Customize the slides to best reflect the needs of the organization and the scope of its planned giving program.

Presentation Formats

Selecting an appropriate format is a critical first step in planning a successful presentation. The format should match the needs of the anticipated audience. Presentations to professional advisors are likely to include more detail and additional information on the more technical aspects of planned giving, whereas presentations to volunteers and friends of the nonprofit are likely to be more informal and less technical.

Each of the various formats has benefits and drawbacks:

- *Lecture.* A lecture format works well for nonprofit boards and committees and for large groups of alumni or friends of the nonprofit. But it can be impersonal and may limit opportunities for interaction between the presenter and the audience.

- *Round table or U-shape workshop.* This option works well for donors, staff, board members, and nonprofit committees because it allows discussion and encourages interaction since all attendees are visible to each other and the presenter. This format also provides ample workspace for participants.

- *Role-playing.* Role-playing can be an effective format for board members or volunteers. Role-playing enhances participation and enables all attendees to get to know each other while learning. It also provides an opportunity for participants to practice solicitations.

- *Case study.* A case study is particularly effective for professional advisors. As discussed later in the section on technical audiences, this format is familiar to attorneys, CPAs, and investment advisors who may have received their continuing education training through the case study method.

ANTICIPATING THE AUDIENCE

To deliver an effective and persuasive presentation that communicates and connects with the audience, it is necessary to consider the presentation from the intended audience's perspective. Consider these questions in adapting presentations to meet the needs of the audience:

- What is the relationship of the audience to the nonprofit?
- What is the audience's level of technical knowledge?
- What does this audience need to know about planned giving?
- Which asset is the audience likely to use to fund gifts?
- What is the anticipated age of the audience?
- Has this audience attended other planned giving presentations?
- Is the presentation structured to offer more than planned giving? For example, some audiences are interested in related topics, such as estate and gift taxes, ways to avoid probate, estate planning, and financial planning.
- How well do members of the audience know each other?
- How well does the audience know the presenter?

PRESENTATIONS TO NONTECHNICAL AUDIENCES

Nontechnical audiences may include the nonprofit's donors, prospects, board members, volunteers, and friends. These audiences appreciate general information about wills, bequests, and income and estate taxation. Planned giving helps these individuals obtain income tax benefits and lifetime streams of income and estate tax reduction. Planned giving is one of the ways to meet this audience's financial needs while providing support to a worthy nonprofit.

PRESENTATIONS TO TECHNICAL AUDIENCES

Technical audiences include professional advisors such as attorneys, trust officers, accountants and investment advisors, and the nonprofit's financial officers. Professional advisors appreciate obtaining information that can assist them in working with their clients. They want information on reducing capital gains taxes, federal estate and gift taxes, trusts, bequests, and estate planning along with information about making gifts of noncash assets such as real estate, securities, and tangible personal property, which may be given outright or used as a way to fund planned gifts. As discussed above, a case study approach, typically used in professional schools, offers a practical and familiar model. Case studies serve as a reference point for these advisors, and speakers can modify this approach to meet the experience level of the audience. A well-designed presentation to professional advisors offers planned giving officers the opportunity to establish themselves with the financial community. These advisors may contact a presenter about a variety of cases and situations, only some of which are likely to benefit the nonprofit organization that sponsors the presentation. However, over time, a number of important gifts may occur that benefit the nonprofit.

The nonprofit's financial officers appreciate learning about the intricacies of planned gifts, especially as they relate to the nonprofit's investment obligation to produce the necessary income to meet payout rates for life income gifts. The information offered to these groups should be broader than just planned giving concepts; the presenter should place planned giving in context with other development programs and with tax, estate, and financial planning concepts.

Audio-Visual Materials

Speaker's Outline

Members of the audience should receive a copy of the speaker's outline and copies of any overheads. For many in the audience, distance from the speaker, poor vision, and poor hearing limit the opportunity to participate in the presentation. A personal set of materials enables each listener to participate more actively in the presentation.

Supplementary Materials

Flipcharts, grease boards, and chalkboards are effective devices for communicating with attendees. In most cases the text should be preprinted on these devices for the presenter's convenience and to avoid delay. These tools summarize information presented and can test the audience's understanding of the information presented.

Computers

At many presentations, it is advantageous for the presenter to bring a laptop or notebook computer to illustrate planned giving calculations. The computer demonstrates the user-friendly nature of most planned giving software programs. Financial calculations can be produced immediately. A well-designed presentation, coupled with calculations tailored to an individual's needs, can open opportunities to discuss potential gift options.

PRESENTATION FORMATS

Overhead Transparencies

Overhead transparencies provide an effective, inexpensive visual medium for the presenter to communicate information and ideas to the audience. To maximize the effectiveness of overheads:

- Use overheads that are either all portrait (vertical), $8\frac{1}{2}''$ wide $\times$ 11" tall, or landscape (horizontal), 11" wide $\times$ $8\frac{1}{2}''$ tall, to orient the attendees to the visual form of communication.

- Select a font that is visually clear and clean. Avoid using script fonts, which are often difficult to read.

- Use a blend of text, charts, and graphs to communicate information.

- Use phrases, brief sentences, or bulleted points, not paragraphs. Text should be limited to emphasize key points. Use numbers or bullets to differentiate between ideas and concepts.

- Place a mark or a colored sticker in the right-hand top corner to help place each overhead correctly.

- Number each overhead and make sure that the number corresponds to the outline or copy of the overhead distributed to the audience. Attendees lose interest when they lose their place.

- Print key concepts or words in advance or print on the overhead during the presentation to emphasize a key point.

Presenters should be careful to position themselves in a way that allows the audience an unobstructed view of the screen. Presenters should face the audience and use a pointer or colored pen to point on the overhead itself, not to the screen. Doing this permits presenters to maintain eye contact with the audience.

PowerPoint Presentations

Many nonprofit organizations use PowerPoint or a similar software to make computer-based presentations. PowerPoint enables presenters to move easily back and forth among slides. The software is attractive, easy to use, and helpful to both presenters and the audience. Give hard copies of the PowerPoint Presentation slides to the audience.

SPEAKING SKILLS

Duration

Presentations may be part of an all-day event at a nonprofit's open house or home-coming program or a one-hour morning or evening session for volunteers. Ideally they should not exceed 40 to 50 minutes in length. Include a question-and-answer session. If there are several sessions, schedule breaks after each presentation. Be sensitive to questions from attendees regarding gift options and discussions about specific assets such as stocks or real estate, which may indicate charitable motivation. Comments by attendees offer insight into the nature, size, and timing of a potential gift and its intended use. Additional staff members should be available to assist attendees and to provide a break to the presenters.

Vocal Delivery and Tone

Vary the tone of speech from soft to loud, brisk to slow, high to low. Avoid a mono-tone or one-dimensional form of speech. Presenters who know the audience can use a conversational and informal tone. Attendees often are fearful that they will not grasp complex and technical information, so consider beginning the presentation with familiar, general information, which helps the audience relax and be ready to learn. Enthusiastic, humorous, and self-effacing speech can disarm listeners.

Speak at a comfortable and conversational pace. A pace that is too fast or slow can be distracting and frustrating to the attendees. Varying the pace also serves to emphasize important points. Use silence to signal the transition from one point to another. Repetition and reinforcement of key concepts and issues is critical to learning. Remember that planned giving concepts are foreign to many attendees, and repetition of concepts reinforces them.

Audience Participation

Each presentation should attempt to involve the audience. One way to do this is to ask, prior to the presentation, a likely attendee for permission to use him or her as a case study. Using one or more attendees from different age brackets as case studies helps to involve all audience members in the presentation. In addition, most people learn and remember more when the planned giving concept is applied to a real-life example. Presenters who are not overly sensitive about their age may use themselves as case studies to introduce benefits of life income gifts.

Practice

Prior to every presentation, practice with the information to be presented. Develop familiar and comfortable opening remarks or anecdotes to help make a connection between the presenter and the audience. Stagefright is caused by inexperience and a lack of confidence in the subject matter of the presentation. Inexperience may be overcome by practice and a lack of confidence can be overcome by knowledge.

Testimonials

An effective way to end a planned giving presentation is to conclude with a testimonial story about a planned giving donor who personifies the meaning of philanthropy. Most organizations have donors who, while not necessarily wealthy, have made a major sacrifice to reach deep into financial reserves to make a planned gift. These testimonials show attendees that they, too, can make significant gifts.

Follow-Up

After the presentation, planned giving staff members should follow up, in writing, with all attendees to thank them for participating in the event. Attendees who indicated a specific interest in a planned gift option should be scheduled for a personal visit, and all attendees should receive future issues of planned giving publications.

Conclusion

Consider these points when making presentations:

- Work to increase knowledge to become comfortable with the planned giving subject matter.
- Practice delivering the key points.
- Never read or memorize a speech. Always work from notes or an outline.
- Never exceed the allotted time.
- Never say anything that could potentially offend any attendee.
- Maintain eye contact.
- Try to spot audience members who look perplexed. Ask questions and review difficult material. Also look for those who appear to understand everything you are saying. With encouragement, they often ask helpful questions or make instructive comments.
- Interact with the audience.
- Leave time for questions at the end.
- Remember, there are prospects at every presentation who are interested in becoming donors.

EXHIBIT 6-1.   MASTER PRESENTATION INVENTORY

This master presentation inventory is contained on the CD-ROM as Document 333. For more information about the subject matter contained on the master presentation inventory, see *Planned Giving: Management, Marketing, and Law, Invest in Charity: A Donor's Guide to Charitable Giving,* or *Planned Giving for Small Nonprofit Organizations,* by Ronald R. Jordan and Katelyn L. Quynn, published by John Wiley & Sons, Inc.

DOCUMENT 333

MASTER PRESENTATION INVENTORY: THUMBNAIL PRESENTATION

Section 1.   Introduction to Planned Giving

Planned Giving: Benefits of Charitable Giving

What Is Planned Giving?

- Mutual benefits to donor and charity
- Gifts through wills and trusts
- Assists donors in making major gifts

Life Income Gifts

- Provide charitable income tax deductions, capital gains avoidance (20%), and estate tax reductions
- Endowments
- Other assets (real estate, stocks, bonds, mutual funds, tangible personal property)
- Financial stability to nonprofit

Planned Giving: Fund Raising versus Development

What Is Fund Raising?

- Outright gifts of cash
- Annual support
- Operating expenses
- Identifies prospects for major gifts

What Is Development?

- Long-term financial support
- Support at all levels
- Multitiered approach to raising money

EXHIBIT 6-1.   MASTER PRESENTATION INVENTORY *(Continued)*

- Integrated approach to raising money
- Development includes planned giving

Why Do Donors Give?

- Involvement with nonprofit
- Contact with staff members or volunteers
- Donative intent
- Philanthropy
- Gifts in honor or in memory
- Repayment of a debt
- Nonprofit as a family substitute
- Tax/financial benefits

GIFT RANGE TABLE FOR A $100,000,000+ CAMPAIGN

Gift	Number of Donors	Amount	Cumulative Total
$15,000,000	1	$ 15,000,000	$ 15,000,000
$10,000,000	2	$20,000,000	$ 35,000,000
$ 5,000,000	3	$ 15,000,000	$ 50,000,000
$ 1,000,000	10	$ 10,000,000	$ 60,000,000
$ 500,000	25	$ 12,500,000	$ 72,500,000
$ 250,000	50	$ 12,500,000	$ 85,000,000
$ 100,000	75	$ 7,500,000	$ 92,500,000
$ 50,000	100	$ 5,000,000	$ 97,500,000
$ 25,000	150	$ 3,750,000	$101,250,000
$ 10,000	250	$ 2,500,000	$103,750,000
$ 1,000	500	$ 500,000	$104,250,000
	Total: 1166		

Types of Planned Gifts

- Life income gifts
  - Charitable gift annuities
  - Deferred gift annuities
  - Pooled income fund
  - Charitable remainder trust
- Gifts from the estate
  - Will
  - Trust

EXHIBIT 6-1.   MASTER PRESENTATION INVENTORY *(Continued)*

- Funds
  - Endowed funds
  - Current-use awards
- Assets other than cash
  - Securities
  - Real estate
  - Nontraditional assets

Section 2.   Life Income Gifts

Life Income Gifts

- Income for the lifetime of donor and/or second beneficiary
- A charitable income tax deduction
- Endowed fund
- Possible avoidance of capital gains taxes
- Leadership club
- A reduction in federal estate taxes

Charitable Gift Annuities

- Income for life paid annually, semiannually, quarterly, or monthly
- A guaranteed return often greater than money market rates (for example, a donor at age ‹YEARS› earns ‹ % ›)
- Immediate charitable income tax deduction
- Reduction in capital gains taxes if the gift is made with appreciated securities
- A chance to support a program of interest
- Membership in a leadership club

BENEFITS OF A $10,000 CHARITABLE GIFT ANNUITY

Age(s)	Rate	Annual Income	Charitable Income Tax Deduction
65	%	$	$
70	%	$	$
75	%	$	$
70/68	%	$	$
75/73	%	$	$

EXHIBIT 6-1. MASTER PRESENTATION INVENTORY *(Continued)*

Deferred Gift Annuities

- An immediate charitable income tax deduction

- Guaranteed income in the future, often at retirement

- An excellent yield (for example, a 40-year old donor who makes a gift of $5,000 earns ‹%› at age 65)

- A reduction in capital gains taxes if the gift is made with appreciated securities

- Membership in a leadership club

BENEFITS OF A $10,000 DEFERRED GIFT ANNUITY*

Age(s)	Rate	Annual Income	Charitable Income Tax Deduction
40	%	$	$
45	%	$	$
50	%	$	$
55	%	$	$
40/45	%	$	$
50/55	%	$	$

*Deferred to Age 65

Pooled Income Fund

- Increase yield
  - (Current rate is ‹ % ›)

- Avoid capital gains tax on gifts of appreciated securities

- Receive an income for life

- Receive an immediate charitable income tax deduction

- Membership in a leadership club

BENEFITS OF A $10,000 POOLED INCOME FUND

Age(s)	Rate	Annual Income	Charitable Income Tax Deduction
60	%	$	$
65	%	$	$
70	%	$	$
70/68	%	$	$
75/73	%	$	$

EXHIBIT 6-1.   MASTER PRESENTATION INVENTORY *(Continued)*

Charitable Remainder Trust Options

- Income to beneficiary for life, remainder to nonprofit
- Charitable Remainder Annuity Trust—fixed payment—invade principal
- Charitable Remainder Unitrust 1: Straight fixed percentage trust—invade principal
- Charitable Remainder Unitrust 2: Net Income Unitrust
- Charitable Remainder Unitrust 3: Net Income Unitrust with a make-up provision

Section 3.   Tax Consequences

Tax Considerations

- The Economic Growth and Tax Relief Reconciliation Act of 2001
- Income Tax Rates:

TIMETABLE FOR MARGINAL INCOME TAX RATE REDUCTIONS

2000	2001*	2002–03	2004–05	2006–10
15%	10%**	10%	10%	10%
	15%	15%	15%	15%
28%	27.5%	27%	26%	25%
31%	30.5%	30%	29%	28%
36%	35.5%	35%	34%	33%
39.6%	39.1%	38.6%	37.6%	35%

*Blended rates for the year that reflect 1% reduction effective July 1, 2001.
**On the first $6,000 of earnings for single filers, $10,000 for heads of households, and $12,000 for married couples, filing jointly.

- Capital Gains: 20% for most investment assets
  - **Example:** Donor purchases stock for $50,000 and one year later the value is $150,000. The gain is $100,000 × 20% = $20,000.
- The donor obtains a charitable income tax deduction for gifts of cash, up to 50%, and for gifts of property, up to 30%, of the donor's adjusted gross income. (Donor must be itemizer; excess may be carried over for up to 5 additional years.)
  - **Example:** Donor makes a gift by check for $75,000 and donor's adjusted gross income is $100,000. The donor may claim a charitable income tax deduction for $50,000 in year one and $25,000 in year two.
- Long-term capital asset defined as an asset held for a year and a day.

EXHIBIT 6-1.   MASTER PRESENTATION INVENTORY *(Continued)*

ESTATE AND GIFT TAX RATES AND UNIFIED CREDIT EXEMPTION AMOUNT

Calendar Year	Estate and GST Tax Deathtime Transfer Exemption	Gift Transfer Exemption Tax	Highest Estate and Gift Tax Rates
2002	$1 million	$1 million	50%
2003	$1 million	$1 million	49%
2004	$1.5 million	$1 million	48%
2005	$1.5 million	$1 million	47%
2006	$2 million	$1 million	46%
2007	$2 million	$1 million	45%
2008	$2 million	$1 million	45%
2009	$3.5 million	$1 million	45%
2010	N/A (taxes repealed)	$1 million	Maximum gift tax rate equal to maximum income tax rate (35%)

- ○ Marital deduction—Unlimited transfers between spouses
- Annual exclusion: $10,000 to each donee/year
  - ○ Husband and wife: $20,000 to each donee/year

Tax Deductibility of Charitable Gifts

- Donor must be an itemizer.
- For gifts of cash, donor obtains charitable income tax deduction limited to 50% of the donor's adjusted gross income and the excess may be carried over for up to 5 years.
  - ○ **Example:** Donor makes a gift by check for $75,000 and donor's adjusted gross income is $100,000. The donor may claim a charitable income tax deduction for $50,000 in year one and $25,000 in year two.
- For gifts of property (other than cash), a donor obtains a charitable income tax deduction equal to the appraised value, limited to 30% of donor's AGI.
- Gifts of real estate and nonmarketable securities must be appraised to ascertain value.
- Gifts of tangible personal property must be appraised (if over $5,000) and have a related use to the exempt purposes of the charity. If so, the donor obtains a charitable income tax deduction equal to the appraised value.

EXHIBIT 6-1.　MASTER PRESENTATION INVENTORY *(Continued)*

Section 4.　Estate Planning—Wills and Trusts

Estate Planning and Charitable Giving

- Financial planning
- Business assets
- Real estate
- Tax law
- Domestic relations
- Charitable gift planning

The Will: A Road Map

- Transfer property from one to another
- Parties to a will: testator, witness, beneficiary, executor
- Formalities
- Codicils
- Updating a will/change in family circumstances—birth, death, divorce, remarriage, relocation
- Executor
- Guardianship
- Distribution of property—individuals and nonprofits

Charitable Provisions

- Specific bequest of cash ($25,000)
- Specific bequest of property
- Residue (all or a specific percentage of the remainder)

Targeting Donors for Bequests

- Bequest programs
- Bequest forms
- Introductory bequest society letter
- Bequest ad
- A "thank you" bequest ad
- Professional advisors

EXHIBIT 6-1. MASTER PRESENTATION INVENTORY *(Continued)*

Coordinating Title to Property with the Estate Plan

- Sole ownership
- Joint ownership with right of survivorship
- Tenancy in common
- Tenancy by the entirety

Probate

- The probate process
- Probate assets—assets owned solely in the name of the decedent
- Nonprobate assets
  - Assets that designate a beneficiary
  - Jointly held property
  - Property transferred to an inter vivos trust

Durable Power of Attorney

- An important estate planning document that grants to another (holder) the power to act on behalf of the grantor.
- The power survives the grantor's incompetence.
- A traditional power of attorney lapses if the grantor becomes incompetent.
- According to the provisions of the durable power, the holder may do any act that the grantor could have conducted in his own right.

Trusts

- Parties—grantor, trustee, beneficiary
- Income versus remainder beneficiaries
- Transferring title to the trust corpus
- Powers governed by the document—buy, sell, mortgage, lease, rent, convey
- Distributions of principal and income
- Special provisions
  - Spray and sprinkle provisions
  - Provisions for minor children
- Charitable provisions

EXHIBIT 6-1. MASTER PRESENTATION INVENTORY *(Continued)*

The Revocable Inter Vivos Trust (Living Trust)

- Lifetime management plan
- Inter vivos transfers—avoid probate
- Testamentary transfers—do not avoid probate
- Revocable—can be amended or revoked; no tax benefits
- Irrevocable—completed transfer subject to gift tax (transferred during life) or estate tax (transferred at death)

Charitable Remainder Trusts

- Income to beneficiary for life, remainder to nonprofit
- Donor obtains a charitable income tax deduction
- Donor avoids capital gains tax on gifts of appreciated property
- Income based on value of assets as revalued annually

BENEFITS OF A $100,000 CHARITABLE REMAINDER TRUST FOR DONOR AGE 70

		Charitable Income Tax Deduction	
Payout Rate	Annual Income	Annuity Trust	Unitrust
5%	$5,000	$	$
6%	$6,000	$	$
7%	$7,000	$	$

Overview of Charitable Remainder Trusts

- Earn 5% to 7% income on your gift.
- Receive an income for life for you and a second beneficiary.
- Receive a charitable income tax deduction.
- Transfer appreciated securities to the trust and avoid capital gains taxes.
- Select your own trustee.
- Select an annuity trust that pays a fixed, guaranteed dollar amount or a unitrust that pays a percentage of the trust as revalued annually.
- Support a program of interest and become a member of a leadership club.

Types of Charitable Remainder Trusts

Annuity Trust

- Fixed dollar amount based on value of initial assets

EXHIBIT 6-1.   MASTER PRESENTATION INVENTORY *(Continued)*

- Invade principal
- No additional gifts

Unitrust (Regular)

- Stated percentage
- Revalued annually
- Invade principal
- Additional gifts

Net Income Unitrust

- Stated % or net income, whichever is less
- Revalued annually
- May not invade principal

Net Income Unitrust with Make-Up

- Stated % or net income, whichever is less with make-up
- Revalued annually
- May not invade principal

Section 5.   Asset Classification

Asset Classification

Cash

Securities

- Stocks
- Bonds
- Mutual funds
- Closely held stock

Real Estate

- Personal residence
- Vacation property or second home
- Farm/ranch
- Commercial property
- Vacant land

EXHIBIT 6-1. MASTER PRESENTATION INVENTORY *(Continued)*

Tangible Personal Property

- Art

- Antiques

- Books

- Collectibles/collections

A Gift of Appreciated Securities

- Donor transfers appreciated securities.

- Donor obtains a charitable income tax deduction equal to the market value of the securities.

- Donor avoids capital gains taxes on the gain in the appreciated securities.

- Donor receives gift credit for the market value of the securities.

Gifts of Closely Held Stock

- Donor transfers closely held stock to nonprofit. Stock must not be restricted so as to prohibit transfer to a third party.

- Closely held stock is not publicly traded. To determine value, the stock must be appraised by one qualified to value business organizations.

- The nonprofit may redeem the stock to a closely held corporation or to the corporation's ESOP and the nonprofit receives a check for the redemption.

- The donor obtains a charitable income tax deduction equal to the appraised value of the stock.

Types of Real Estate

- Personal residence

- Farm or ranch

- Commercial property

- Vacation property

- Second home

Gifts of Real Estate

- Guidelines

EXHIBIT 6-1. MASTER PRESENTATION INVENTORY *(Continued)*

- Considerations in accepting gifts of real estate
- Types of real estate
- Tax considerations
- Gift options
- Outright gift or gift of a fractional interest
- Retained life estate
- Charitable Remainder Unitrust

Guidelines for Real Estate Gifts

- Nonprofits should not assume the role of a substitute buyer
- Nonprofits need to establish safeguards and procedures (environmental audit)
- Nonprofits should not become an unwitting recipient of damaged goods
- If the buyer cannot sell the property, how can the nonprofit?

Considerations in Accepting Gifts of Real Estate

- Treating the gift as a sale
- Appraisal
- Gift review committee
- Gift brokering
- Gifts of mortgaged property

Gift Options for Real Estate

- Outright gifts and gifts of a fractional interest
- Retained life estate
- Charitable Remainder Unitrust

Outright Gift of Real Estate or a Gift of Fractional Interest

- Appraised value
- Cost basis
- Donor obtains a charitable income tax deduction equal to the appraised value, limited to 30% of adjusted gross income

---

EXHIBIT 6-1.   MASTER PRESENTATION INVENTORY *(Continued)*

Retained Life Estate

- Donor age 75 owns a personal residence. Donor wishes to make a gift of the personal residence and retains the right to live in the home for life.
  - Appraised value   ‹$›
- Benefits to donor
  - Charitable income tax deduction of   ‹$›
  - Right to occupy the property for life
- A gift of a personal residence or farm
- Donor obtains a charitable income tax deduction based on the appraised value of the property and the age of the donor
- Donor is responsible for maintenance, insurance, and taxes

Charitable Remainder Unitrust (Net Income Unitrust with Make-Up Provision)

- Donor and spouse age 65 own vacant land or commercial property and wish to make a gift. Donors select the payout rate and receive a charitable income tax deduction and an income stream for their lifetimes, and avoid capital gains taxes on the appreciation of the assets. The property passes outside of the estate for federal estate tax purposes and avoids probate.

APPRAISED VALUE $500,000		COST BASIS $250,000
	Income Stream	Tax Deduction
5%	$25,000	$
6%	$30,000	$
7%	$35,000	$

Gifts of Tangible Personal Property

- Gifts of tangible personal property must have a use related to the exempt purposes of the nonprofit organization.
- Charitable income tax deduction equal to fair market value (appraised value) if there is a related use.
- Charitable income tax deduction is limited to the cost basis if there is no related use.
- For property donated for resale, the charitable income tax deduction is limited to the cost basis.
- For property that an author or artist donates, which if sold would produce ordinary income, the charitable income tax deduction is limited to the donor's cost basis (cost of materials).

EXHIBIT 6-1.   MASTER PRESENTATION INVENTORY *(Continued)*

Section 6.   Building Endowments

Establish a Named Endowed Fund

- Operate in perpetuity
- Award income annually
- May be established in the donor's name, family member as a memorial fund
- Benefit any designated department, program, or activity
- Support research, education, or scholarships

Establishing a Scholarship

- Endowed
- Current use
- In memory or in honor
- Funded with a gift of cash, securities, or real estate through an outright gift, planned gift, or gift by will or trust

## CHAPTER 7

IRS Forms and Documents

Introduction

This chapter focuses exclusively on Internal Revenue Service (IRS) forms and related documents and is divided into charitable remainder annuity trusts, charitable remainder unitrusts, and pooled income funds. The charitable remainder annuity trusts and unitrusts are further divided into trusts that pay out to a single beneficiary or to two or more beneficiaries who may receive payments concurrently or consecutively.

Most of the documents are ones that the IRS has "approved." So long as taxpayers (and their advisors) substantially follow the sample document, they can be assured that the IRS will recognize their submission as having met all the necessary requirements. The samples are considered safe harbors, and donors and their attorneys may rely on them, knowing they will not be challenged.

Review all boilerplate documents carefully to make certain that they and their provisions are appropriate for the particular circumstances and needs of the donor. Because the sample documents are generic, they apply to general sets of circumstances and a wide variety of cases. Be careful not to use the wrong form for a specific case. Attorneys who specialize in charitable gift planning and estates and trusts modify these forms to meet the specific needs of their clients. Donors should be cautioned (along with their attorneys if they do not regularly represent donors on charitable gift matters) about the blanket use of these documents. Also, you should be sure to read the **Important Reminder** from the Internal Revenue Service (regarding charitable remainder trust model forms) which is posted on page 139.

Documents

This chapter and the documents included in Section 7 of the CD-ROM focus exclusively on Tax and IRS Documents. The CD-ROM contains 53 documents that perform the functions described in this chapter. In addition the following documents are specifically referenced and included in this chapter:

Document 382   Charitable Remainder Annuity Trust
Document 376   Charitable Remainder Unitrust
Document 420   Declaration of Trust for a Pooled Income Fund
Document 421   Instrument of Transfer for a Pooled Income Fund

CHARITABLE REMAINDER ANNUITY TRUSTS

Charitable remainder annuity trusts pay an annuity amount equal to a stated percentage of the net fair market value of the trust's assets (see Exhibit 7-1). The appendix and CD-ROM contain several different forms for charitable remainder annuity trusts. Select the correct one depending on the number of beneficiaries and whether they will be paid concurrently or consecutively.

EXHIBIT 7-1.   CHARITABLE REMAINDER ANNUITY TRUST

This is a sample charitable remainder annuity trust. Compare the language in the payout clause with that of the charitable remainder unitrust that appears in Exhibit 7-2. This language clearly illustrates the difference between these two types of trusts.

DOCUMENT 382

CHARITABLE REMAINDER ANNUITY TRUST

IRS Form: Rev. Proc. 89-21

Section 4. Sample Charitable Remainder Annuity Trust

On this ‹***› day of ‹***›, I, ‹***› (hereinafter referred to as "the Donor") desiring to establish a charitable remainder annuity trust, within the meaning of Rev. Proc. 89-21 and section 664(d)(1) of the Internal Revenue Code (hereinafter referred to as "the Code") hereby create the ‹***› Charitable Remainder Annuity Trust ("the Trust") and designate ‹***› as the initial Trustee.

1. *Funding of Trust.* The Donor transfers to the Trustee the property described in Schedule A, and the Trustee accepts such property and agrees to hold, manage, and distribute such property of the Trust under the terms set forth in this Trust instrument.

2. *Payment of Annuity Amount.* The Trustee shall pay to ‹A LIVING INDIVIDUAL› (hereinafter referred to as "the Recipient") in each taxable year of the Trust during the

EXHIBIT 7-1.   CHARITABLE REMAINDER ANNUITY TRUST *(Continued)*

Recipient's life an annuity amount equal to ‹AT LEAST FIVE› percent of the net fair market value of the assets of the Trust as of this date. The annuity amount shall be paid in equal quarterly amounts from income and, to the extent income is not sufficient, from principal. Any income of the Trust for a taxable year in excess of the annuity amount shall be added to principal. If the net fair market value of the Trust assets is incorrectly determined, then within a reasonable period after the value is finally determined for Federal tax purposes, the Trustee shall pay to the Recipient (in the case of an undervaluation) or receive from the Recipient (in the case of an overvaluation) an amount equal to the difference between the annuity amount(s) properly payable and the annuity amount(s) actually paid.

3. *Proration of the Annuity Amount.* In determining the annuity amount, the Trustee shall prorate the same on a daily basis for a short taxable year and for the taxable year of the Recipient's death.

4. *Distribution to Charity.* Upon the death of the Recipient, the Trustee shall distribute all of the then principal and income of the Trust (other than any amount due Recipient or Recipient's estate under paragraphs 2 and 3, above) to ‹***› (hereinafter referred to as the Charitable Organization). If the Charitable Organization is not an organization described in sections 170(c), 2055(a), and 2522(a) of the Code at the time when any principal or income of the Trust is to be distributed to it, then the Trustee shall distribute such principal or income to such one or more organizations described in sections 170(c), 2055(a), and 2522(a) as the Trustee shall select in its sole discretion.

5. *Additional Contributions.* No additional contributions shall be made to the Trust after the initial contribution.

6. *Prohibited Transactions.* The income of the Trust for each taxable year shall be distributed at such time and in such manner as not to subject the Trust to tax under section 4942 of the Code. Except for the payment of the annuity amount to the Recipient, the Trustee shall not engage in any act of self-dealing, as defined in section 4941(d), and shall not make any taxable expenditures, as defined in section 4945(d). The Trustee shall not make any investments that jeopardize the charitable purpose of the Trust, within the meaning of section 4944, or retain any excess business holdings, within the meaning of section 4943.

7. *Successor Trustee.* The Donor reserves the right to dismiss the Trustee and to appoint a successor Trustee.

8. *Taxable Year.* The taxable year of the Trust shall be the calendar year.

9. *Governing Law.* The operation of the Trust shall be governed by the laws of the State of ‹***›. However, the Trustee is prohibited from exercising any power or discretion

---

EXHIBIT 7-1.   CHARITABLE REMAINDER ANNUITY TRUST *(Continued)*

---

granted under said laws that would be inconsistent with the qualification of the Trust under section 664(d)(1) of the Code and the corresponding regulations.

10. *Limited Power of Amendment.* The Trust is irrevocable. However, the Trustee shall have the power, acting alone, to amend the Trust in any manner required for the sole purpose of ensuring that the Trust qualifies and continues to qualify as a charitable remainder annuity trust within the meaning of section 664(d)(1) of the Code.

11. *Investment of Trust Assets.* Nothing in this Trust instrument shall be construed to restrict the Trustee from investing the Trust assets in a manner that could result in the annual realization of a reasonable amount of income or gain from the sale or disposition of Trust assets.

IN WITNESS WHEREOF ‹***› and ‹TRUSTEE› by its duly authorized officer have signed this agreement the day and year first above written.

_____
‹DONOR›

_____
‹TRUSTEE›

By _____
‹ACKNOWLEDGMENTS, WITNESSES, ETC.›

CHARITABLE REMAINDER UNITRUSTS

Charitable remainder unitrusts pay a unitrust amount in one of the following three ways:

1. *Unitrust Form 1 Straight Fixed Percentage.* This unitrust pays an amount equal to the straight fixed percentage of the net fair market value of the trust's assets as revalued annually.

2. *Unitrust Form 2 Net Income Unitrust.* This trust pays the lesser of the straight fixed percentage and the actual net income of the trust.

3. *Unitrust Form 3 Net Income Unitrust with a Make-Up Provision.* This trust pays the lesser of the straight fixed percentage and the actual net income of the trust but makes up any shortfall between the net income and the fixed percentage in any year where the trust has net income that exceeds the straight fixed percentage.

Donors and their advisors should select the most appropriate form of charitable remainder unitrust depending on the donor's situation and the type of asset used to fund the trust (see Exhibit 7-2).

EXHIBIT 7-2. SAMPLE CHARITABLE REMAINDER UNITRUST

This is a sample charitable remainder unitrust. This trust pays a straight fixed percentage of the net fair market value of the trust's assets as valued annually.

DOCUMENT 376

CHARITABLE REMAINDER UNITRUST

IRS Form: Rev. Proc. 89-20

Section 4. Sample Charitable Remainder Unitrust

On this ‹***› day of ‹***›, 20 ‹***›, I (hereinafter referred to as "the Donor"), desiring to establish a charitable remainder unitrust, within the meaning of Rev. Proc. 89-20 and section 664(d)(2) of the Internal Revenue Code (hereinafter referred to as "the Code") hereby create the ‹***› Charitable Remainder Unitrust and designate ‹***› as the initial Trustee.

1. *Funding of Trust.* The Donor transfers to the Trustee the property described in Schedule A, and the Trustee accepts such property and agrees to hold, manage, and distribute such property of the Trust under the terms set forth in this Trust instrument.

2. *Payment of Unitrust Amount.* The Trustee shall pay to ‹A LIVING INDIVIDUAL› (hereinafter referred to as "the Recipient") in each taxable year of the Trust during the Recipient's life a unitrust amount equal to ‹AT LEAST FIVE› percent of the net fair market value of the assets of the Trust valued as of the first day of each taxable year of the Trust (the "valuation date"). The unitrust amount shall be paid in equal quarterly amounts from income and, to the extent that income is not sufficient, from principal. Any income of the Trust for a taxable year in excess of the unitrust amount shall be added to principal. If the net fair market value of the Trust assets is incorrectly determined, then within a reasonable period after the value is finally determined for Federal tax purposes, the Trustee shall pay to the Recipient (in the case of an undervaluation) or receive from the Recipient (in the case of an overvaluation) an amount equal to the difference between the unitrust amount properly payable and the unitrust amount actually paid.

3. *Proration of the Unitrust Amount.* In determining the unitrust amount, the Trustee shall prorate the same on a daily basis for a short taxable year and for the taxable year of the Recipient's death.

4. *Distribution to Charity.* Upon the death of the Recipient, the Trustee shall distribute all of the then principal and income of the Trust (other than any amount due Recipient or Recipient's estate, under paragraphs 2 and 3, above) to ‹***› (hereinafter referred to as the Charitable Organization). If the Charitable Organization is not an

EXHIBIT 7-2. SAMPLE CHARITABLE REMAINDER UNITRUST *(Continued)*

organization described in sections 170(c), 2055(a), and 2522(a) of the Code at the time when any principal or income of the Trust is to be distributed to it, then the Trustee shall distribute such principal or income to such one or more organizations described in sections 170(c), 2055(a), and 2522(a) as the Trustee shall select in its sole discretion.

5. *Additional Contributions.* If any additional contributions are made to the Trust after the initial contribution, the unitrust amount for the year in which the additional contribution is made shall be ‹THE SAME PERCENTAGE AS IN PARAGRAPH 2› percent of the sum of (a) the net fair market value of the Trust assets as of the first day of the taxable year (excluding the assets so added and any income from, or appreciation on, such assets) and (b) that proportion of the value of the assets so added that was excluded under (a) that the number of days in the period that begins with the date of contribution and ends with the earlier of the last day of the taxable year or the Recipient's death bears to the number of days in the period that begins on the first day of such taxable year and ends with the earlier of the last day in such taxable year or the Recipient's death. In the case where there is no valuation date after the time of contribution, the assets so added shall be valued at the time of contribution.

6. *Prohibited Transactions.* The income of the Trust for each taxable year shall be distributed at such time and in such manner as not to subject the Trust to tax under section 4942 of the Code. Except for the payment of the unitrust amount to the Recipient, the Trustee shall not engage in any act of self-dealing, as defined in section 4941(d), and shall not make any taxable expenditures, as defined in section 4945(d). The Trustee shall not make any investments that jeopardize the charitable purpose of the Trust, within the meaning of section 4944, or retain any excess business holdings, within the meaning of section 4943.

7. *Successor Trustee.* The Donor reserves the right to dismiss the Trustee and to appoint a successor Trustee.

8. *Taxable Year.* The taxable year of the Trust shall be the calendar year.

9. *Governing Law.* The operation of the Trust shall be governed by the laws of the State of ‹***›. However, the Trustee is prohibited from exercising any power or discretion granted under said laws that would be inconsistent with the qualification of the Trust under section 664(d)(2) of the Code and the corresponding regulations.

10. *Limited Power of Amendment.* The Trust is irrevocable. However, the Trustee shall have the power, acting alone, to amend the Trust in any manner required for the sole purpose of ensuring that the Trust qualifies and continues to qualify as a charitable remainder unitrust within the meaning of section 664(d)(2) of the Code.

EXHIBIT 7-2.   SAMPLE CHARITABLE REMAINDER UNITRUST *(Continued)*

---

11.   *Investment of Trust Assets.* Nothing in this Trust instrument shall be construed to restrict the Trustee from investing the Trust assets in a manner that could result in the annual realization of a reasonable amount of income or gain from the sale or disposition of Trust assets.

IN WITNESS WHEREOF ‹***› and ‹TRUSTEE› by its duly authorized officer have signed this agreement the day and year first above written.

‹DONOR›

‹TRUSTEE›

By _____

‹ACKNOWLEDGMENTS, WITNESSES, ETC.›

POOLED INCOME FUNDS

A number of documents in Section 7 of the CD-ROM pertain to gifts to a pooled income fund. Documents 415–425 are generally administrative documents regarding pooled income funds.

Two of the most common documents associated with pooled income funds are the Sample Declaration of Trust, which establishes the trust, and the Instrument of Transfer, which enables donors to contribute to the fund.

Declaration of Trust

Taxpayers who make transfers to a trust that substantially follows this sample instrument are assured that the IRS will recognize the trust as meeting all of the requirements of a qualified pooled income fund. The trust must operate in a manner consistent with the terms of the trust and qualify as a valid trust under local law (see Exhibit 7-3).

EXHIBIT 7-3.   DECLARATION OF TRUST FOR A POOLED INCOME FUND

This sample form meets IRS requirements. All pooled income funds are established with this document.

EXHIBIT 7-3.   DECLARATION OF TRUST FOR A POOLED
INCOME FUND *(Continued)*

DOCUMENT 420

POOLED INCOME FUND

IRS Form: Rev. Proc. 88-53

Section 4. Sample Declaration of Trust

On this ‹***› day of ‹***›, 20‹***›, the Board of Trustees of the ‹***› Public Charity (hereinafter referred to as "Public Charity") desiring to establish a pooled income fund within the meaning of Rev. Proc. 88-53 and section 642(c)(5) of the Internal Revenue Code (hereinafter referred to as "the Code"), hereby creates the ‹***› Public Charity Pooled Income Fund (hereinafter referred to as "the Fund") and designates ‹***› as the initial trustee to hold, manage, and distribute such property hereinafter transferred to and accepted by it as part of the Fund under the following terms and conditions.

1.   *Gift of Remainder Interest.* Each donor transferring property to the Fund shall contribute an irrevocable remainder interest in such property to Public Charity.

2.   *Retention of Life Income Interest.* Each donor transferring property to the Fund shall retain for himself or herself an income interest in the property transferred, or create an income interest in such property for the life of one or more named beneficiaries, provided that each income beneficiary must be a living person at the time of the transfer of property to the Fund by the donor. If more than one beneficiary of the income interest is named, such beneficiaries may enjoy their shares concurrently and/or consecutively. Public Charity may also be designated as one of the beneficiaries of the income interest. The donor need not retain or create a life interest in all of the income from the property transferred to the Fund and any income not payable to an income beneficiary shall be contributed to, and within the taxable year of the Fund in which it is received paid to, Public Charity.

3.   *Commingling of Property.* The property transferred to the Fund by each donor shall be commingled with, and invested or reinvested with, other property transferred to the Fund by other donors satisfying the requirements of this instrument and of section 642(c)(5) of the Code or corresponding provision of any subsequent federal tax law. The Fund shall not include property transferred under arrangements other than those specified in this instrument and satisfying the said provisions of the Code.

All or any portion of the assets of the Fund may, however, be invested or reinvested jointly with other properties not a part of the Fund that are held by, or for the use of, Public Charity. When joint investment or reinvestment occurs, detailed accounting records shall be maintained by the Trustee specifically identifying the

EXHIBIT 7-3. DECLARATION OF TRUST FOR A POOLED INCOME FUND *(Continued)*

portion of the jointly invested property owned by the Fund and the income earned by, and attributable to, such portion.

4. *Prohibition against Exempt Securities.* The property transferred to the Fund by any donor shall not include any securities whose income is exempt from taxation under subtitle A of the Code or the corresponding provisions of any subsequent federal tax law. The Trustee of the Fund shall not accept or invest in such securities as part of the assets of the Fund.

5. *Maintenance by Public Charity.* Public Charity shall always maintain the Fund or exercise control, directly or indirectly, over the Fund. Public Charity shall always have the power to remove any Trustee or Trustees and to designate a new Trustee or Trustees.

6. *Prohibition against Donor or Beneficiary Serving as Trustee.* The Fund shall not have as a Trustee a donor to the Fund or a beneficiary (other than Public Charity) of an income interest in any property transferred to the Fund. No donor or beneficiary (other than Public Charity) shall have, directly or indirectly, general responsibilities with respect to the Fund that are ordinarily exercised by a Trustee.

7. *Income of Beneficiary to Be Based on Rate of Return of Fund.* The taxable year of the Fund shall be the calendar year. The Trustee shall pay income to each beneficiary entitled thereto in any taxable year of the Fund in the amount determined by the rate of return earned by the Fund for the year with respect to the beneficiary's income interest. Payments must be made at least once in the year in which the income is earned. Until the Trustee determines that payments shall be made more or less frequently or at other times, the Trustee shall make income payments to the beneficiary or beneficiaries entitled to them in four quarterly payments on or about March 31, June 30, September 30, and December 31 of each year. An adjusting payment, if necessary, will be made during the taxable year or within the first 65 days following its close to bring the total payment to the actual income to which the beneficiary or beneficiaries are entitled for that year.

On each transfer of property by a donor to the Fund, there shall be assigned to the beneficiary or beneficiaries of the income interest retained or created in the property the number of units of participation equal to the number obtained by dividing the fair market value of the property transferred by the fair market value of a unit in the Fund immediately before the transfer. The fair market value of a unit in the Fund immediately before the transfer shall be determined by dividing the fair market value of all property in the Fund at the time by the number of units then in the Fund. The initial fair market value of a unit in the Fund shall be the fair market value of the property transferred to the Fund divided by the number of units

EXHIBIT 7-3.   DECLARATION OF TRUST FOR A POOLED
INCOME FUND *(Continued)*

assigned to the beneficiaries of the income interest in that property. All units in the Fund shall always have equal value.

If a transfer of property to the Fund by a donor occurs on other than a determination date, the number of units of participation assigned to the beneficiary or beneficiaries of the income interest in the property shall be determined by using the average fair market value of the property in the Fund immediately before the transfer, which shall be deemed to be the average of the fair market values of the property in the Fund on the determination dates immediately preceding and succeeding the date of transfer. For the purpose of determining the average fair market value, the property transferred by the donor and any other property transferred to the Fund between the preceding and succeeding dates, or on such succeeding date, shall be excluded. The fair market value of a unit in the Fund immediately before the transfer shall be determined by dividing the average fair market value of the property in the Fund at that time by the number of units then in the Fund. Units of participation assigned with respect to property transferred on other than a determination date shall be deemed to be assigned as of date of the transfer.

A determination date means each day within a taxable year of the Fund on which a valuation is made of the property in the Fund. The property of the Fund shall be valued on January 1, April 1, July 1, and October 1 of each year; provided, however, that where such date falls on a Saturday, Sunday, or legal holiday (as defined in section 7503 of the Code and the regulations thereunder), the valuation shall be made on the next succeeding day which is not a Saturday, Sunday, or legal holiday.

The amount of income allocated to each unit of participation in the Fund shall be determined by dividing the income of the Fund for the taxable year by the outstanding number of units in the Fund at the end of the year, except that income shall be allocated to units outstanding during only part of the year by taking into consideration the period of time the units are outstanding during the year.

For purposes of this instrument, the term "income" has the same meaning as it does under section 643(b) of the Code or corresponding provision of any subsequent federal tax law and the regulations thereunder.

The income interest of any beneficiary of the Fund shall terminate with the last regular payment of income that was made before the death of the beneficiary. The Trustee of the Fund shall not be required to prorate any income payment to the date of the beneficiary's death.

8. *Termination of Life Income Interest.* Upon the termination of the income interest of the designated beneficiary (or, in the case of successive income interests, the survivor of the designated beneficiaries) entitled to receive income pursuant to the

EXHIBIT 7-3.   DECLARATION OF TRUST FOR A POOLED
INCOME FUND *(Continued)*

terms of a transfer to the Fund, the Trustee shall sever from the Fund an amount equal to the value of the remainder interest in the property upon which the income interest is based. The value of the remainder interest for severance purposes shall be its value as of the date on which the last regular payment was made before the death of the beneficiary. The amount so severed from the Fund shall be paid to Public Charity. If at the time of severance of the remainder interest Public Charity has ceased to exist or is not a public charity (an organization described in clauses (i) through (vi) of section 170(b)(1)(A) of the Code), the amount severed shall be paid to an organization selected by the Trustee that is a public charity.

9. *Prohibited Activities.* The income of the Fund for each taxable year shall be distributed at such time and in such manner as not to subject the Fund to tax under section 4942 of the Code. Except for making the required payments to the life income beneficiaries, the Trustee shall not engage in any act of self-dealing as defined in section 4941(d) and shall not make any taxable expenditures as defined in section 4945(d). The Trustee shall not make any investments that jeopardize the charitable purpose of the Fund within the meaning of section 4944 or retain any excess business holdings within the meaning of section 4943.

10. *Depreciable or Depletable Assets.* The Trustee shall not accept or invest in any depreciable or depletable assets.

11. *Incorporation by Reference.* The provisions of this document may be, and are intended to be, incorporated by reference in any will, trust, or other instrument by means of which property is transferred to the Fund. Any property transferred to the Fund whereby an income interest is retained or created for the life of one or more named beneficiaries, where this document is not incorporated by reference, shall become a part of the Fund and shall be held and managed under the terms and conditions of this document, unless the instrument of transfer is inconsistent with such terms and conditions, in which case the Trustee shall not accept the property.

12. *Governing Law.* The operation of the Fund shall be governed by the laws of the State of ‹***›. However, the Trustee is prohibited from exercising any power or discretion granted under said laws that would be inconsistent with the qualification of the Fund under section 642(c)(5) of the Code and the corresponding regulations.

13. *Power of Amendment.* The Fund is irrevocable. However, Public Charity shall have the power, acting alone, to amend this document and the associated instruments of transfer in any manner required for the sole purpose of ensuring that the Fund qualifies and continues to qualify as a pooled income fund within the meaning of section 642(c)(5).

EXHIBIT 7-3.   DECLARATION OF TRUST FOR A POOLED
INCOME FUND *(Continued)*

IN WITNESS WHEREOF ‹PUBLIC CHARITY› and ‹TRUSTEE› by their duly authorized officers have signed this agreement the day and year first above written.

‹PUBLIC CHARITY›

By _____
‹TRUSTEE›

By _____
‹ACKNOWLEDGMENTS, WITNESSES, ETC.›

Instruments of Transfer

Pooled income funds use instruments of transfer to enable donors to transfer property, to make provisions for income payments, and to distribute the remainder interest to a nonprofit organization (see Exhibit 7-4).

EXHIBIT 7-4.   INSTRUMENT OF TRANSFER FOR A POOLED
INCOME FUND

This instrument of transfer for a pooled income fund is for a single beneficiary. The donor and the charity should complete the parts of the form describing the property transferred, the payout, and the designation of the remainder to charity.

DOCUMENT 421

POOLED INCOME FUND

IRS Form: Rev. Proc. 88-53

SECTION 5. Sample Instrument of Transfer: One Life

On this ‹***› day of ‹***›, 20‹***›, I hereby transfer to the ‹***› Public Charity Pooled Income Fund, under the terms and conditions set forth in its Declaration of Trust, the following property: ‹***›.

The income interest attributable to the property transferred shall be paid as follows:

A. To me during my lifetime.

B. To ‹***› during his or her life. However, I reserve the right to revoke, solely by will, this income interest.

EXHIBIT 7-4.   INSTRUMENT OF TRANSFER *(Continued)*

Upon the termination of the income interest, the Trustee of the Fund will sever from the Fund an amount equal to the value of the remainder interest in the transferred property and transfer it to Public Charity:

A. For its general uses and purposes.

B. For the following charitable purpose(s): ‹***›. However, if it is not possible for Public Charity in its sole discretion to use the severed amount for the specified purpose(s), then it may be used for the general purposes of Public Charity. This instrument and the transfer of property made pursuant thereto shall be effective after acceptance by both Donor and the Trustee.

IN WITNESS WHEREOF ‹***› and ‹TRUSTEE› by its duly authorized officer have signed this agreement the day and year first above written.

‹DONOR›

‹TRUSTEE›

By _____

‹ACKNOWLEDGMENTS, WITNESSES, ETC.›

CONCLUSION

This chapter focuses on a number of documents used to establish charitable remainder annuity trusts, charitable remainder unitrusts, and pooled income funds. The CD-ROM contains the documents most commonly used for these gift options. Because the documents are, by definition, samples, each needs to be evaluated and selected based on the particular gift situation involved. Then these forms must be reviewed for appropriateness by experienced legal counsel and revised accordingly.

Important Reminder

At the time this book went into production, the Internal Revenue Service was considering issuing revised charitable remainder trust model forms. Once issued, readers should obtain copies of these documents and ask the nonprofit organization's general counsel or other outside legal counsel to evaluate the impact of these changes on forms currently being used and also on forms contained within this text. Please remember that all CD-ROM documents need to be modified to reflect the current tax law and the ever-changing discount rate.

Appendix (and CD-ROM)

The *Planned Giving Workbook* comes with a CD-ROM containing 425 documents that relate to the chapters within the book. The documents on the CD-ROM are all customizable, so that they can be tailored to fit the specific requirements of any organization.

To give readers a sense of what is included on the CD-ROM, this appendix includes several sample documents from each of the seven main subject areas.

Section 1: Marketing Materials

Document 15	Ad: Scholarship Funded through Bequest
Document 35	Buckslip: Gifts of Tangible Personal Property
Document 44	Column: Establishing a Named Scholarship
Document 72	Fact Sheet: Gifts of Appreciated Securities

Section 2: Agreements

Document 78	Agreement: Establish Reunion Fund Gift
Document 106	Agreement: Endowed Chair
Document 120	Agreement: Qualified Contributions of Inventory for the Needy
Document 124	Agreement: Deed of Gift

Section 3: Correspondence

Document 132	Letter: Standard Acknowledgment from Asset Manager
Document 145	Letter: Life Income Follow-Up
Document 188	Letter: Gift of Tangible Personal Property and Calculation of Charitable Income Tax Deduction
Document 213	Letter: Follow-Up on Donor's Inquiry

Section 4: Administrative Documents

Section 5: Exhibits

Section 6: Presentations

Section 7: IRS Forms and Tax-Related Documents

WHAT'S ON THE CD-ROM?

Here is a breakdown of the 425 documents included on the CD-ROM according to subject area.

Section 1: Marketing Materials

Section 2: Agreements

AD: SCHOLARSHIP FUNDED THROUGH BEQUEST

You Can Establish a Scholarship at <ORGANIZATION>

Would you like to establish a scholarship or prize at <ORGANIZATION>? Have you always thought you could not afford it? Consider funding a scholarship or prize through a bequest, which is an amount of money or a percentage of your estate that you leave to the <ORGANIZATION> in your will. A minimum of < $ > is needed to fund an endowed scholarship. Through a bequest you can:

- Make a gift through your estate while preserving the funds you need to live on
- Reduce your federal estate taxes
- Make an enduring contribution to <ORGANIZATION>
- Become a member of the <PLANNED GIVING SOCIETY>

The Office of Development would like to explain how you can make a bequest to <ORGANIZATION>. Contact <NAME>, <TITLE>, <ADDRESS>, <CITY, STATE ZIP>; <TELEPHONE>.

BUCKSLIP: GIFTS OF TANGIBLE PERSONAL PROPERTY

<ORGANIZATION>

A Gift of Tangible Personal Property to <ORGANIZATION>

You can make a gift of tangible personal property, such as art, antiques, or collectibles, to <ORGANIZATION>. Gifts of these assets can provide attractive benefits to donors while offering valuable tangible personal property to <ORGANIZATION>:

- Donor transfers tangible personal property to <ORGANIZATION>.

- Gifts of tangible personal property should have a use related to the exempt purposes of <ORGANIZATION>.

- If the property has a related use, the donor obtains a charitable income tax deduction equal to the appraised value of the property.

- If there is no related use, the donor obtains a charitable income tax deduction equal to the donor's cost basis.

If you want to learn how a gift of tangible personal property can benefit you and <ORGANIZATION>, call the Office of Planned Giving. Please contact <NAME>, <TITLE>, at <ADDRESS>, <CITY, STATE ZIP>; <TELEPHONE>.

DOCUMENT 44

COLUMN: ESTABLISHING A NAMED SCHOLARSHIP

Establishing a Named Scholarship

Endowed Scholarship

Endowed scholarship funds provide much-needed financial assistance to worthy and needy students at ‹ORGANIZATION›.

Scholarship funds can be tailored to meet your specific goals. First, you must decide whom you're trying to benefit. You may choose to provide assistance to a student studying a specific major or in a particular program at ‹ORGANIZATION›. You may decide whether the recipient should be a graduate or an undergraduate, and whether the candidate must be financially needy and academically worthy to receive the award.

You must also decide how to fund the scholarship. The minimum level at ‹ORGANIZA-TION› is ‹ $ › to establish a named endowed scholarship fund. You may fund it now with cash or fund it partially or completely through a planned gift or through a bequest from your estate. If you establish the fund now, you have the opportunity to be recognized for your participation and will be able to meet the recipient.

Your named fund can grow with the help of friends and family. Additional gifts can be made by you at any time. Often relatives and friends make gifts in lieu of birthday or holiday presents.

Current-Use Scholarships

An alternative to an endowed scholarship is a current-use fund. Current-use scholarship funds are spent in the year the gift is made and are for unrestricted scholarship purposes. These funds do not grow but provide financial assistance to ‹ORGANIZATION› students. You can create a named current-use scholarship for as little as ‹ $ ›. Why not enable a deserving student to benefit from the educational opportunities at ‹ORGANIZATION›?

For information about establishing a scholarship fund, please contact ‹ORGANIZATION›, ‹NAME›, ‹TITLE›, ‹ADDRESS›, ‹CITY, STATE ZIP› or call ‹TELEPHONE›.

FACT SHEET: GIFTS OF APPRECIATED SECURITIES

Gifts of Appreciated Securities

A gift of appreciated securities to ‹ORGANIZATION› can greatly benefit a donor by providing tax benefits through a charitable income tax deduction. A gift of appreciated securities through a life income gift provides increased income to the donor compared with CD rates or average stock dividends and diminishes capital gains taxes while providing a charitable income tax deduction.

Outright Gifts of Appreciated Securities

Long-term appreciated securities are stocks or bonds that have been owned for at least a year and a day and have increased in value. Making a gift of appreciated securities benefits a donor in two ways: the donor receives a charitable income tax deduction for the full fair market value of the securities and at the same time avoids capital gains taxes on the appreciated securities. The gain is measured by the difference between the cost basis (the amount originally paid for the stock) and its current fair market value.

Benefits of a Gift of Appreciated Securities

- Donor transfers appreciated securities
- Donor obtains a charitable income tax deduction equal to the market value of the securities
- Donor avoids capital gains taxes on gain of the appreciated securities
- Donor receives gift credit for market value of the securities

Guidelines for Gifts of Appreciated Securities

If you have physical possession of the stock certificates, you should send the certificates (unendorsed) in one envelope and signed stock powers, with a signature guarantee from your bank, in another envelope. If you do not have physical possession and your broker has the securities in a "street account," then we can work with you and your broker to transfer the stock electronically or through DTC instructions to ‹ORGANIZATION›.

For more information, please feel free to contact ‹NAME›, Director of Planned Giving at ‹ORGANIZATION› Office of Planned Giving, ‹ADDRESS, CITY, STATE ZIP› or call ‹TELEPHONE›. We will be happy to assist you in making a gift to benefit ‹ORGANIZATION›.

AGREEMENT: ESTABLISH REUNION FUND GIFT

Reunion Class Prize Fund Description
The Class of ‹YEAR› Endowed Prize Fund

‹ORGANIZATION› and the Class of ‹YEAR› hereby propose to establish the Class of ‹YEAR› Endowed Prize Fund at ‹ORGANIZATION› in accordance with the wishes of the donors, the Class of ‹YEAR›. The fund shall be established through cash and planned gifts.

‹STATEMENT ABOUT THE CLASS OF _____ ›

The fund is defined and administered as follows:

The title of the fund shall be the Class of ‹YEAR› Endowed Prize Fund at College of ‹COLLEGE NAME›. The income shall be used to make an annual award to a full-time graduate or undergraduate student. The fund shall benefit a student studying at the College of ‹COLLEGE NAME›.

Eligible candidates must have a demonstrated financial need and solid academic standing. Selection of candidates shall be made by the Office of Financial Aid in consultation with the Dean of the College of ‹COLLEGE NAME›.

If in the judgment of the Executive Committee of ‹ORGANIZATION› it becomes impossible to accomplish the purposes of this gift, the income or principal, or both, may be used in such manner as determined by the Executive Committee of ‹ORGANIZATION›.

_____

Date

_____

Date

_____

On behalf of the Class of ‹YEAR›
College of ‹COLLEGE NAME›

_____

‹TITLE›
For ‹ORGANIZATION›

AGREEMENT: ENDOWED CHAIR

The ‹DONOR'S NAME› Endowed Chair at the ‹ORGANIZATIONAL DEPARTMENT›

‹ORGANIZATION›

‹ORGANIZATION› and the ‹DONOR NAME› family hereby propose to establish the ‹DONOR› Endowed Chair at the ‹ORGANIZATIONAL DEPARTMENT› at ‹ORGANIZATION› in accordance with the wishes of the donors. The Chair shall be devoted to ‹PURPOSE OF CHAIR› in the ‹SPECIFIC AREA›.

The Chair is defined and administered as follows: The title of the Chair shall be the ‹TITLE›. Income from this gift shall be used to provide support to the holder of the Chair in the form of salary, staff support, and expenses associated with the Chair. In any year in which there is no one eligible to be holder of this Chair, any income not distributed shall be added to principal or accumulated for future use. The Chair shall be funded through a gift of ‹ $ › from ‹DONOR›. This fund may be augmented with cash gifts in the future.

The ‹DONOR'S NAME› has been ‹DESCRIBE RELATIONSHIP TO ORGANIZATION›. The establishment of this Chair recognizes the valuable contributions of the ‹DONOR NAME› family to the ‹ORGANIZATION› and recognizes the ‹DONOR'S NAME› contribution to education as the founder and director of ‹DONOR'S ORGANIZATION›. In addition, this Chair pays tribute to the ‹DONOR'S› years of dedicated service to the ‹NAME› community in establishing a ‹NAME› establishment that provides quality products and benefits the community by providing innovations and opportunities into ‹AREA OF INTEREST›.

If in the judgment of the ‹COMMITTEE› of ‹ORGANIZATION› it becomes impossible to accomplish the purposes of this gift, the income or principal, or both, may be used in such manner as determined by the ‹COMMITTEE› of the ‹ORGANIZATION›.

_____	_____
Date	‹DONOR›
_____	_____
Date	‹DONOR›
_____	_____
Date	‹ORGANIZATION›

AGREEMENT: QUALIFIED CONTRIBUTIONS
OF INVENTORY FOR THE NEEDY

Qualified Contributions—Gifts for the Ill,
Needy, and Infants

‹DONOR NAME›, ‹C!TY, STATE ZIP› has today, ‹DATE›, transferred to ‹ORGANIZATION› of ‹CITY, STATE ZIP› ‹QUANTITY AND DESCRIPTION OF PROPERTY TRANSFERRED› and consistent with the Internal Revenue Service procedures the ‹NONPROFIT› warrants the following:

1. The property has a use related to the exempt purposes of the donee.

2. The property will be used by the donee solely for the care of the ill, the needy, or infants.

3. The property has not been transferred to the donee in exchange for money, other property, or services.

_____   _____
Date   ‹DONOR›
                                    ‹NAME OF NONPROFIT REPRESENTATIVE›

DOCUMENT 124

DEED OF GIFT

Deed of Gift

‹ORGANIZATION›

DONOR: _____
          Name(s)

ADDRESS: _____
          Street

          _____
          City, State Zip

I /We, ‹NAME OF DONOR(S)›, represent and guarantee that I/we is/are the lawful owners of the property described below, that it is free of all encumbrances, and that I/we have the right to give or transfer the legal title to the following property to ‹ORGANIZATION›: ‹ADD DESCRIPTION OF PROPERTY›

I (We) declare the appraised value of the above listed property(s) on this date as $_____.

_____   _____
Donor Signature   Date   Donor Signature   Date

STATE OF _____, COUNTY OF _____

The foregoing instrument was acknowledged before me this ____ day of _____, 20__.

My commission expires: _____   _____
                                                  NOTARY PUBLIC

Acceptance of Gift

_____ on behalf of ‹ORGANIZATION›, accept the legal title of the gift from ‹NAME OF DONOR(S)›, donor(s), of the above described property.

_____   _____
Signature   Title   Date

STATE OF _____, COUNTY OF _____

The foregoing instrument was acknowledged before me this ____ day of _____, 20__.

My commission expires: _____   _____
                                                  NOTARY PUBLIC

DOCUMENT 132

LETTER: STANDARD ACKNOWLEDGMENT FROM ASSET MANAGER

‹DATE›

‹RETURN ADDRESS›

Dear Mr. ‹NAME›:

We acknowledge receipt of your gift to the ‹ORGANIZATION› Pooled Life Income Fund summarized below:

Date of Gift:	‹DATE›
Type of Gift:	‹SECURITIES, CASH, OTHER›
Value of Gift:	$ ‹ $ ›
Number of Units:	‹NUMBER›

The income beneficiary associated with your gift to the Pooled Income Fund is:

Name:	‹NAME›
Terms:	Income to income beneficiary for life

The charitable deduction you may declare for federal income tax purposes is ‹ $ ›. This is supported by the enclosed report.

We note also your instructions to ‹NAME OF CONTACT› that the remainder interest be used to benefit the ‹DESCRIPTION OF PURPOSE›.

For the ‹ORGANIZATION› Pooled Income Fund, I welcome you as a Pooled Income Fund participant. Please feel free to contact me if you have questions at ‹TELEPHONE NUMBER›.

Sincerely,

Account Manager
Asset Management Company

DOCUMENT 145

LETTER: LIFE INCOME FOLLOW-UP

‹DATE›

‹NAME›
‹ADDRESS›
‹CITY, STATE ZIP›

Dear ‹NAME›:

Greetings from the ‹ORGANIZATION› Office of Development. Your support of ‹ORGANIZA-TION› and its programs provides valuable assistance, and your gifts make you an important member of the ‹ORGANIZATION› community.

We want to thank you once again for your support and let you know that our staff is available to assist you in achieving your tax, estate planning, and charitable giving objectives.

You may be interested in learning the benefits of a new Charitable Gift Annuity. With a gift of ‹ $ › calculated at your age of ‹AGE›, you receive a charitable income tax deduction of ‹ $ › with an annuity rate of ‹ % ›, which produces an annual income of ‹ $ ›. As you know, you may receive the income on an annual, monthly, or quarterly basis, and you may designate your gift to benefit one of your areas of interest.

Please call me at ‹TELEPHONE› to set up an appointment if you are interested in further information. Thank you for your continued support.

Sincerely,

‹NAME›
‹TITLE›

DOCUMENT 188

LETTER: GIFT OF TANGIBLE PERSONAL PROPERTY AND CALCULATION OF CHARITABLE INCOME TAX DEDUCTION

‹DATE›

‹NAME›
‹ADDRESS›
‹CITY, STATE ZIP›

Dear ‹NAME›:

Thanks for the information about the gift of equipment. The charitable income tax deduction is determined based on the nature of the property in the hands of the donor. Based on our discussion, the property is equipment in the hands of the donor and is classified as tangible personal property with a related use to the exempt purposes of ‹ORGANIZATION›. As such, the general rule is that the charitable income tax deduction is based on the appraised value of the property but must be reduced by the amount of any depreciation claimed.

We advise all donors who make these types of gifts to consult with their tax or legal advisors.

If I can be of further help, please feel free to call me at ‹TELEPHONE›.

Sincerely,

‹NAME›
‹TITLE›

ABC:abc

LETTER: FOLLOW-UP ON DONOR'S INQUIRY

‹DATE›

‹NAME›
‹ADDRESS›
‹CITY, STATE ZIP›

Dear ‹NAME›:

‹ORGANIZATION› means many things to students, faculty, staff, and alumni. ‹ORGANIZA-TION› means educational opportunity, strong academic programs, state-of-the-art computers, teaching laboratories, and enrichment programs in arts, music, and recreation. Charitable gifts provide essential financial resources to ‹ORGANIZATION›. In return, donors receive favorable charitable income tax deductions and the good feeling that comes from philanthropy—one person helping another.

Some time ago you requested information on charitable gift planning opportunities at ‹ORGANIZATION›. I hope the information provided was helpful to you. The goal of the ‹OFFICE OF PLANNED GIVING› is to provide service to donors, alumni, and friends who would like to learn more about the attractive mutual benefits that gifts can provide to ‹ORGANIZA-TION› and the donor.

We hope that if you have questions, you will call us. In the meantime, please find enclosed a newsletter that provides an overview of some of our most popular charitable gift planning options. Please contact me at ‹TELEPHONE› if I can be of further assistance.

Sincerely,

‹NAME›
‹TITLE›

ABC:abc
Enclosure: Newsletter

EXHIBIT: PLANNED GIVING ASSISTANT:
ANNOUNCEMENT OF POSITION

Announcement of Position Availability

Title:	Planned Giving Assistant
Employer:	Reports to <TITLE>
Effective Date:	<DATE>
Salary:	Competitive Salary

Qualifications:

- Bachelor's degree required.

- A minimum of 3 years experience preferred in the fields of banking, law, financial planning, or accounting or related fields.

- Candidate must demonstrate the following skills and abilities:

  1. Ability to work with donors as part of a team

  2. Ability to forge strong working relationships with others and have a capacity for engendering confidence and trust

  3. Exceptional interpersonal and communication skills

  4. High motivation level and consistent follow-through

  5. Technical proficiency

Responsibilities:

- Produce planned giving financial calculations.

- Develop training materials demonstrating the benefits of planned giving options and use of various assets.

- Produce marketing materials for planned giving.

- Conduct research to identify planned giving prospects.

- Provide technical support and planned giving assistance.

Benefits Offered: <LIST BENEFITS>.

Deadline for Applications: Submit cover letter and resume by <DATE>.

Apply to: <NAME, TITLE>
           <ORGANIZATION>
           <ADDRESS>
           <CITY, STATE ZIP>

EXHIBIT: PLANNED GIVING ACTION PLAN FOR CAMPAIGN

Timeline

Year 1 Quiet Phase ‹$ GOAL› Activities	Year 2 Kickoff ‹$ GOAL› Activities	Year 3 Public Phase ‹$ GOAL› Activities	Year 4 ‹$ GOAL› Activities
1. Screen Prospects	1. Kickoff Celebration	1. Solicit Planned Gifts	1. Faculty/Staff
2. Finalize Campaign Needs	2. Sequential Solicitation	2. Campaign Leadership	2. Planned Gifts Wrap-Up
3. Print Marketing Materials	3. Regional Events/ Programs	3. Regional Events/ Programs	3.
4. Develop Leadership Structure	4. Contact Professional Advisors	4.	4.
5. Organize Presentations	5. Symposiums	5.	5.
6. Organize Planned Giving Committee	6.	6.	6.
7. Build Nucleus Fund	7.	7.	7. Victory Celebration
Planning	**Planning**	**Planning**	**Planning**
1. Prepare for Kickoff Celebration	1. Faculty/Staff Planning	1. Faculty/Staff Planning	1. Campaign Closure
2. Invite Planned Gift Prospects	2. Prospect Identification	2. Prospect Identification	2. Integration of Strategic Plan
3.	3.	3.	3. Post-Campaign Fund Raising
4. Identify Top Prospects	4.	4.	4. Phase II Campaign Planning
5. Assign Top Prospects	5.	5.	5.
6. Identify Professional Advisors	6.	6.	6.

FORM: MANAGEMENT REPORT TOP 100 DONORS

‹ORGANIZATION›

Management Report Top 100 Donors

Last Name	Full Name	Zip	Amount	Date	Project	Staff

DOCUMENT 271

FORM: GIFT ADMINISTRATION FORM

COMPLETE ❐

Gift Administration Form

Donor ID #: _____

Name: _____

Address: _____

City: _____

SS# _____   D.O.B. _____

Second Beneficiary: _____

Address: _____

City: _____

SS# _____   D.O.B. _____

Type of Gift:

❐ HIF   ❐ BIF   ❐ CGA   ❐ DGA   ❐ CRT

Date of Gift:

❐ **Securities**   ❐ **Cash**

   Amount: $_____   Amount: $_____

   Cost basis _____

   Company/# of shares _____

❐ Check/Securities received   ❐ Sent to Asset Manager

   Date: _____   Date: _____

❐ Instrument of Transfer/Gift Annuity Contract/Trust Document signed and sent to donor

❐ Instrument of Transfer/Gift Annuity Contract/Trust Document signed and sent to Asset Manager

❐ Calculations and confirmation from Asset Manager

❐ Acknowledgment letter sent to donor

   ❐ Development officer thank-you   from: _____

   ❐ Tax receipt   from: _____

   ❐ Special acknowledgment   from: _____

❐ Pledge Form completed

DOCUMENT 312

EXHIBIT: SAMPLE RECEIPT AND RELEASE FORM

Surrogate's Court of the State of ‹ STATE›—‹ COUNTY› County

Accounting by
‹ EXECUTOR/TRIX› , as Executor(trix)
of the Estate of ‹DECEDENT›, Deceased

RECEIPT AND RELEASE

FILE NUMBER ‹NUMBER›

The undersigned, being of full age, sound mind, and under no disability, and entitled to share in the estate of the above-named decedent, as a legatee under a will,

(a)   Acknowledges that each fiduciary named above has fully and satisfactorily accounted for all assets of the Estate;

(b)   Acknowledges receipt of money paid as follows:

money (cash or check) ‹ $ ›

(c)   The foregoing payment is in full payment of

[X] a legacy, under Article ‹ARTICLE NUMBER› (c) of the Will;
[ ] a claim against the estate;
[ ] the amount directed to be paid by a decree of this court dated _____,
20____ ;
[ ] other: [specify]

(d)   Releases and discharges each fiduciary named above from all liability to the under-signed for any and all matters relating to or derived from the administration of the estate; waives the issuance and service of a citation to attend any and all proceed-ings for the judicial settlement of the account; and authorizes the Surrogate to make and enter a decree settling the account and fully releasing and discharging each fiduciary named above as to all matters embraced therein.

Dated: ‹DATE›_____

‹CHARITY›_____
Name

‹NAME AND TITLE OF OFFICER›_____
Name and title of officer

‹SIGNATURE›_____
Signature

‹ADDRESS OF CHARITY›_____
Address

DEFERRED GIFT ANNUITY
ANNUAL INCOME AND CHARITABLE INCOME
TAX DEDUCTION FOR A SINGLE BENEFICIARY
FOR A GIFT OF $10,000 FOR A DONOR WHO
DEFERS PAYOUT TO POINTS IN THE FUTURE

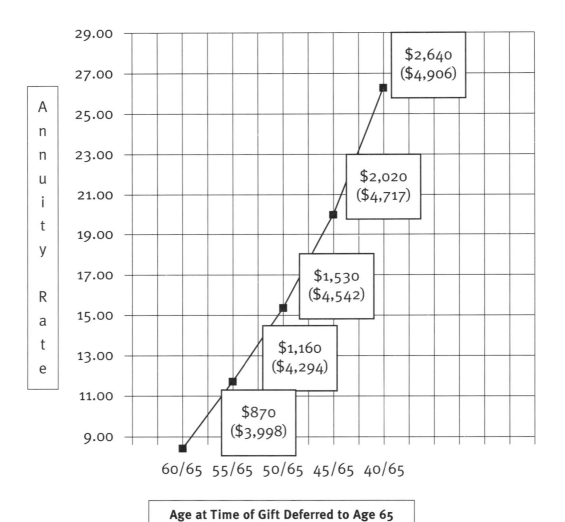

Note: Actual deductions and rates are affected by prevailing discount rates and payout rates recommended by the American Council on Gift Annuities.

EXHIBIT: AUGMENTING ENDOWED FUNDS

Building Your Endowed Family Fund

Over the years the Office of Development has helped families increase the size of their endowed family funds, and we are pleased to share with you some of our ideas. We welcome the opportunity to develop a plan to increase your family fund to provide additional benefits to the ‹PROGRAMS› at ‹ORGANIZATION›.

Please consider the following ideas that have been successfully used to augment family funds:

- Make an annual gift to the fund. Over time such annual gifts may double the size of your family fund.
- Honor family members' birthdays, anniversaries, and weddings by making gifts to the fund in their names.
- Some families, in lieu of exchanging birthday or holiday presents, make a gift to the family fund.
- Make a planned gift and designate your gift to benefit your family fund.
- Through your will, leave a percentage of your estate or a specific dollar amount to your fund.
- Let friends, colleagues, and relatives know of your fund and invite their support.
- For memorial services, suggest that in lieu of flowers or fruit, gifts be made to your family fund at ‹ORGANIZATION›, ‹ADDRESS, CITY, STATE ZIP›.

We welcome your suggestions.

For further information, please contact:
‹NAME›
‹TITLE›
‹ORGANIZATION›
‹ADDRESS›
‹CITY, STATE ZIP›
‹TELEPHONE›

DOCUMENT 327

EXHIBIT: AVAILABILITY AND COST OF LONG-TERM CARE

Worksheet to record information when investigating which agencies and facilities provide long-term care services in our area (or in the area where you would be most likely to receive care) and what the costs are for these services.

Home Health Agency

Name of *one* Home Health Agency your agency might use

Name of *another* Home Health Agency you might use

_____

_____

_____

Address _____

_____

_____

Phone Number _____

Contact Person _____

_____

_____

_____

Address _____

_____

_____

Phone Number _____

Contact Person _____

Check which types of care are available and list the cost

Skilled Nursing Care

Cost/Visit $_____

Home Health Care

Cost/Visit $_____

Personal/Custodial

Cost/Visit $_____

Home Care Services

Cost/Visit $_____

Skilled Nursing Care

Cost/Visit $_____

Home Health Care

Cost/Visit $_____

Personal/Custodial

Cost/Visit $_____

Home Care Services

Cost/Visit $_____

PRESENTATION: POOLED INCOME FUND

Pooled Income Fund

- Increase current yield (current rate is ‹ % ›)
- Avoid capital gains tax on gifts of appreciated securities
- Receive an income for life
- Receive an immediate charitable income tax deduction
- Become a member of a leadership club

BENEFITS OF A $10,000 POOLED INCOME FUND GIFT

Age(s)	Rate	Annual Income	Charitable Income Tax Deduction
60	%	$	$
65	%	$	$
70	%	$	$
70/68	%	$	$
75/73	%	$	$

PRESENTATION: THE WILL: A ROAD MAP

The Will: A Road Map

- Transfer property from one to another
- Parties to a will: testator, witness, beneficiary, executor
- Formalities
- Codicils
- Updating a will/change in family circumstances—birth, death, divorce, remarriage, relocation
- Executor
- Guardianship
- Distribution of property—individuals and nonprofits

PRESENTATION: TARGETING DONORS FOR BEQUESTS

Targeting Donors for Bequests

- Bequest programs
- Bequest forms
- Introductory bequest society letter
- Bequest ad
- A "thank you" bequest ad
- Professional advisors

PRESENTATION: OVERVIEW OF CHARITABLE REMAINDER TRUSTS

Overview of Charitable Remainder Trusts

- Earn 5% to 7% income on gift
- Receive an income for life for donor and a second beneficiary
- Receive a charitable income tax deduction
- Transfer appreciated securities to the trust and avoid capital gains taxes
- Select own trustee
- Select an annuity trust that pays a fixed, guaranteed dollar amount or a unitrust that pays a percentage of the trust as revalued annually
- Support a program that interests you and become a member of a leadership club

CHARITABLE REMAINDER ANNUITY TRUST

Rev. Proc. 89-21(5) — Application

The Service will recognize a trust as meeting all of the requirements of a qualified charitable remainder annuity trust under section 664(d)(1) of the Code if the trust instrument makes reference to this document and is substantially similar to the sample provided in section 4, provided the trust operates in a manner consistent with the terms of the trust instrument and provided it is a valid trust under applicable local law. A trust that contains substantive provisions in addition to those provided by section 4 (other than provisions necessary to establish a valid trust under applicable local law) or that omits any of these provisions will not necessarily be disqualified, but neither will it be assured of qualification under the provisions of this revenue procedure.

CHARITABLE REMAINDER UNITRUST

Rev. Proc. 90-31(3)—Scope and Objective

The sample forms of trust meet all of the applicable requirements of section 664(d)(2) and (3) of the Code and include:

Sec. 4—Sample Inter Vivos Charitable Remainder Unitrust: One Life;

Sec. 5—Sample Inter Vivos Charitable Remainder Unitrust: Two Lives, Consecutive Interests;

Sec. 6—Sample Inter Vivos Charitable Remainder Unitrust: Two Lives, Concurrent and Consecutive Interests;

Sec. 7—Sample Testamentary Charitable Remainder Unitrust: One Life;

Sec. 8—Sample Testamentary Charitable Remainder Unitrust: Two Lives, Consecutive Interests; and

Sec. 9—Sample Testamentary Charitable Remainder Unitrust: Two Lives, Concurrent and Consecutive Interests.

In all cases, the termination of the life interests must be followed by distribution of the trust assets to the charitable remainder beneficiary, and the trust must be a valid trust under applicable local law.

If the trust provisions are substantially similar to those in one of the samples provided in sections 4 through 9, the Service will recognize the trust as satisfying all of the applicable requirements of section 664(d)(2) and (3) of the Code and the corresponding regulations. A document will be considered to be substantially similar to one of the samples even though, for example, the wording is varied to comport with local law and practice as necessary to create trusts, define legal relationships, pass property by bequest, provide for the appointment of alternative and successor trustees, or designate alternative charitable remaindermen. Moreover, for transfers to a qualifying charitable remainder unitrust, the remainder interest will be deductible under sections 170(f)(2)(A), 2055(e)(2)(A), and 2522(c)(2)(A) for income, estate, and gift tax purposes, respectively, if the charitable remainder beneficiary otherwise meets all of the requirements of those provisions. Therefore, it will not be necessary for a taxpayer to request a ruling on the qualification of a substantially similar trust. A trust that contains substantive provisions in addition to those provided by sections 4 through 9 (other than provisions necessary to establish a valid trust under applicable local law) or that omits any of these provisions will not necessarily be disqualified, but it will not be assured of qualification under the provisions of this revenue procedure.

POOLED INCOME FUND

Rev. Proc. 88-53(2)—Background

The Internal Revenue Service receives and responds to requests for rulings dealing with the qualification of trusts as pooled income funds and the availability of deductions for contributions made to such trusts. In many of these requests, the trust investments and charitable objectives are very similar. Consequently, in order to provide a service to taxpayers and to save the time and expense involved in requesting and processing a ruling on a proposed pooled income fund, taxpayers who make transfers to a trust that substantially follows the sample trust instrument contained herein can be assured that the Service will recognize the trust as meeting all of the requirements of a qualified pooled income fund, provided the trust operates in a manner consistent with the terms of the trust instrument and provided it is a valid trust under applicable local law.

LIST OF CD-ROM DOCUMENTS

#	Name of Document	Directory	Subdirectory	Type
1	Ways to Give	Marketing	Planned Giving Brochure	Brochure
2	Planned Giving Mini-Guide	Marketing	Planned Giving Brochure	Brochure
3	A Guide to Planned Giving	Marketing	Planned Giving Brochure	Brochure
4	Professional Advisors Committee Resource Manual	Marketing	Planned Giving Brochure	Brochure
5	Creating an Endowed Fund through Charitable Giving	Marketing	Planned Giving Brochure	Brochure
6	Conservation Easements	Marketing	Ad for Organization Publications	Ad
7	To Promote Office of Planned Giving	Marketing	Ad for Organization Publications	Ad
8	Planned Giving Office	Marketing	Ad for Organization Publications	Ad
9	Gift of Appreciated Securities	Marketing	Ad for Organization Publications	Ad
10	Charitable Gift Annuity Administration	Marketing	Ad for Organization Publications	Ad
11	Deferred Gift Annuity	Marketing	Ad for Organization Publications	Ad
12	Testimonial (Deferred Gift Annuity)	Marketing	Ad for Organization Publications	Ad
13	Charitable Remainder Trust	Marketing	Ad for Organization Publications	Ad
14	Life Income Gifts	Marketing	Ad for Organization Publications	Ad
15	Scholarship Funded through Bequest	Marketing	Ad for Organization Publications	Ad
16	Gift of Real Estate	Marketing	Ad for Organization Publications	Ad
17	Tangible Personal Property	Marketing	Ad for Organization Publications	Ad
18	Gifts through an Estate	Marketing	Ad for Organization Publications	Ad
19	Sidebar Ad Questioning Will	Marketing	Ad for Organization Publications	Ad
20	Gifts of Nontraditional Assets	Marketing	Ad for Organization Publications	Ad
21	Gift of a Collection	Marketing	Ad for Organization Publications	Ad
22	Thank You for a Bequest/Planned Giving Society	Marketing	Ad for Organization Publications	Ad
23	Response Form	Marketing	Planned Giving Buckslip	Buckslip
24	To Promote Office of Development	Marketing	Planned Giving Buckslip	Buckslip
25	Planned Giving Office	Marketing	Planned Giving Buckslip	Buckslip
26	Tax Tips	Marketing	Planned Giving Buckslip	Buckslip
27	Pooled Income Fund	Marketing	Planned Giving Buckslip	Buckslip
28	Charitable Gift Annuities	Marketing	Planned Giving Buckslip	Buckslip

LIST OF CD-ROM DOCUMENTS *(Continued)*

#	Name of Document	Directory	Subdirectory	Type
29	Deferred Gift Annuities	Marketing	Planned Giving Buckslip	Buckslip
30	Charitable Remainder Trust	Marketing	Planned Giving Buckslip	Buckslip
31	Testimonial (Deferred Gift Annuity)	Marketing	Planned Giving Buckslip	Buckslip
32	Life Income Gifts	Marketing	Planned Giving Buckslip	Buckslip
33	Establishing Scholarships	Marketing	Planned Giving Buckslip	Buckslip
34	Gifts of Real Estate	Marketing	Planned Giving Buckslip	Buckslip
35	Gifts of Tangible Personal Property	Marketing	Planned Giving Buckslip	Buckslip
36	Gifts through an Estate	Marketing	Planned Giving Buckslip	Buckslip
37	Gift to Hospital in Honor or Memory	Marketing	Planned Giving Buckslip	Buckslip
38	Establishing an Endowed Fund	Marketing	Planned Giving Buckslip	Buckslip
39	Deferred Gift Annuities	Marketing	Planned Giving Buckslip	Buckslip
40	Gifts of Appreciated Securities	Marketing	Columns for Organization Publication	Column
41	Closely Held Stock	Marketing	Columns for Organization Publication	Column
42	Charitable Remainder Trust	Marketing	Columns for Organization Publication	Column
43	Life Income Gifts	Marketing	Columns for Organization Publication	Column
44	Establishing a Named Scholarship	Marketing	Columns for Organization Publication	Column
45	Real Estate Gifts	Marketing	Columns for Organization Publication	Column
46	Gifts of Insurance	Marketing	Columns for Organization Publication	Column
47	Funding the Cost of Tuition	Marketing	Columns for Organization Publication	Column
48	Interest Rates	Marketing	Columns for Organization Publication	Column
49	Tax Resolutions	Marketing	Columns for Organization Publication	Column
50	Sample Annual Report Page of Planned Giving Information	Marketing	Columns for Organization Publication	Column
51	Establishing an Endowed Fund	Marketing	Planned Giving Newsletter	Newsletter
52	A Menu of Planned Giving Options	Marketing	Planned Giving Newsletters	Newsletter
53	Charitable Gift Annuities and Pooled Income Funds	Marketing	Planned Giving Newsletters	Newsletter
54	Younger to Middle-Aged Prospects	Marketing	Planned Giving Newsletters	Newsletter
55	Life Income Gifts	Marketing	Planned Giving Newsletters	Newsletter
56	Gifts of Real Estate	Marketing	Planned Giving Newsletters	Newsletter

LIST OF CD-ROM DOCUMENTS *(Continued)*

#	Name of Document	Directory	Subdirectory	Type
57	Estate Planning	Marketing	Planned Giving Newsletters	Newsletter
58	Tangible Personal Property	Marketing	Planned Giving Newsletters	Newsletter
59	To Promote Charitable Remainder Trusts	Marketing	Planned Giving Newsletters	Newsletter
60	The Economic Growth and Tax Relief Reconciliation	Marketing	Planned Giving Newsletters	Newsletter
61	Charitable Gift Annuities	Marketing	Planned Giving Newsletters	Newsletter
62	Response Mechanism—Generic	Marketing	Response Forms	Form
63	Response Mechanism—Life Income Gift	Marketing	Response Forms	Form
64	Response Form—Gift of Real Estate	Marketing	Response Forms	Form
65	Building Your Endowed Family Fund	Marketing	Fact Sheet	Fact Sheet
66	Charitable Gift Annuities	Marketing	Fact Sheet	Fact Sheet
67	Charitable Remainder Trusts	Marketing	Fact Sheet	Fact Sheet
68	Deferred Gift Annuity	Marketing	Fact Sheet	Fact Sheet
69	Establishing an Endowed Fund	Marketing	Fact Sheet	Fact Sheet
70	The Pooled Income Fund	Marketing	Fact Sheet	Fact Sheet
71	Estate Planning	Marketing	Fact Sheet	Fact Sheet
72	Gifts of Appreciated Securities	Marketing	Fact Sheet	Fact Sheet
73	Gifts of Real Estate	Marketing	Fact Sheet	Fact Sheet
74	Life Income Gifts	Marketing	Fact Sheet	Fact Sheet
75	Gifts of Tangible Personal Property	Marketing	Fact Sheet	Fact Sheet
76	Addendum to an Endowed Scholarship Fund	Agreement	Endowed Funds	Agreement
77	Addendum to Amend Endowment Agreement	Agreement	Endowed Funds	Agreement
78	Establish Reunion Fund Gift	Agreement	Endowed Funds	Agreement
79	Memorial Prize Fund	Agreement	Endowed Funds	Agreement
80	Memorial Scholarship Fund	Agreement	Endowed Funds	Agreement
81	Endowed Fund for Award	Agreement	Endowed Funds	Agreement
82	Multiple-Purpose Endowed Fund	Agreement	Endowed Funds	Agreement
83	Endowed Memorial Scholarship Fund	Agreement	Endowed Funds	Agreement
84	Addendum to Previous Scholarship Fund	Agreement	Endowed Funds	Agreement

#	Name of Document	Directory	Subdirectory	Type
85	Agreement to Establish a Scholarship Umbrella Fund	Agreement	Endowed Funds	Agreement
86	Endowment Agreement to Support Multiple Purposes	Agreement	Endowed Funds	Agreement
87	Endowed Excellence Fund	Agreement	Endowed Funds	Agreement
88	Endowment Funded by Structured Gift	Agreement	Endowed Funds	Agreement
89	The Presidential Excellence Endowment Fund	Agreement	Endowed Funds	Agreement
90	Endowed Fund Description: Geriatrics	Agreement	Endowed Funds	Agreement
91	Fund Description: Renovating Facilities	Agreement	Endowed Funds	Agreement
92	Fund Description: Patient Advocacy	Agreement	Endowed Funds	Agreement
93	Sample Permanently Restricted Endowed Fund Description	Agreement	Endowed Funds	Agreement
94	Sample Board Designated Endowed Fund Description	Agreement	Endowed Funds	Agreement
95	‹Donor› Endowed Scholarship Fund in ‹Department› at ‹Organization›	Agreement	Endowed Funds	Agreement
96	Professional Development and Travel Endowment	Agreement	Endowed Funds	Agreement
97	Current-Use Award	Agreement	Current-Use Awards	Agreement
98	Current-Use Scholarship Award	Agreement	Current-Use Awards	Agreement
99	Current-Use Award	Agreement	Current-Use Awards	Agreement
100	Sample Current-Use Form	Agreement	Current-Use Awards	Agreement
101	Chair	Agreement	Chairs/Professorships	Agreement
102	Endowed Chair	Agreement	Chairs/Professorships	Agreement
103	Endowed Chair of Legal Studies	Agreement	Chairs/Professorships	Agreement
104	Endowed Professorship	Agreement	Chairs/Professorships	Agreement
105	Chair 2	Agreement	Chairs/Professorships	Agreement
106	Endowed Chair	Agreement	Chairs/Professorships	Agreement
107	One-Beneficiary Charitable Gift Annuity	Agreement	Life Income Gifts	Agreement
108	Charitable Gift Annuity Distribution for One Beneficiary	Agreement	Life Income Gifts	Agreement
109	Two-Beneficiary Gift Annuity	Agreement	Life Income Gifts	Agreement
110	Charitable Gift Annuity Distribution for Two Beneficiaries	Agreement	Life Income Gifts	Agreement
111	Deferred Gift Annuity Agreement for One Beneficiary	Agreement	Life Income Gifts	Agreement
112	Deferred Gift Annuity Agreement for Two Beneficiaries	Agreement	Life Income Gifts	Agreement

LIST OF CD-ROM DOCUMENTS *(Continued)*

#	Name of Document	Directory	Subdirectory	Type
113	Subsequent Gift Agreement	Agreement	Life Income Gifts	Form
114	To Accept a Gift of Stock from Donor	Agreement	Securities	Agreement
115	Agreement to Accept a Gift of Real Estate	Agreement	Real Estate	Agreement
116	Memorandum of Understanding for Gift of Real Estate	Agreement	Real Estate	Agreement
117	Retained Life Estate	Agreement	Real Estate	Agreement
118	Form for Deed with Retained Life Estate	Agreement	Real Estate	Agreement
119	Qualified Contributions of Inventory for Research	Agreement	Nontraditional Assets	Agreement
120	Qualified Contributions of Inventory for the Needy	Agreement	Nontraditional Assets	Agreement
121	Transfer of Work of Art and Copyright	Agreement	Nontraditional Assets	Agreement
122	Memorandum of Understanding Regarding Collection	Agreement	Nontraditional Assets	Agreement
123	Curation Agreement for a Collection	Agreement	Nontraditional Assets	Agreement
124	Deed of Gift	Agreement	Miscellaneous	Agreement
125	Legally Binding Pledge Agreement	Agreement	Miscellaneous	Agreement
126	To Donors Who Make Securities Gifts/Pooled Income Funds	Correspondence	Life Income Gifts	Letter
127	Comparing Benefits of Charitable Gift Annuity and Deferred Gift Annuity	Correspondence	Life Income Gifts	Letter
128	Advising Donor about Deferred Gift Annuity Benefits/Endowed Fund	Correspondence	Life Income Gifts	Letter
129	Comparing the Benefits of a Charitable Gift Annuity for Different Amounts and Clarifying the Standard Deduction	Correspondence	Life Income Gifts	Letter
130	Substantiation for a Charitable Gift Annuity	Correspondence	Life Income Gifts	Letter
131	Substantiation for a Pooled Income Fund Gift	Correspondence	Life Income Gifts	Letter
132	Standard Acknowledgment from Asset Manager	Correspondence	Life Income Gifts	Letter
133	Asset Manager's Mutual Fund Instruction Letter	Correspondence	Life Income Gifts	Letter
134	Gift Acknowledgment	Correspondence	Life Income Gifts	Letter
135	Charitable Gift Annuity for One Beneficiary	Correspondence	Life Income Gifts	Letter
136	Charitable Gift Annuity and Dististribution Agreement for Approval (Enclosures)	Correspondence	Life Income Gifts	Letter
137	Charitable Gift Annuity for Two Beneficiaries	Correspondence	Life Income Gifts	Letter
138	Charitable Gift Annuity—Thank You to Donor	Correspondence	Life Income Gifts	Letter

#	Name of Document	Directory	Subdirectory	Type
139	Deferred Gift Annuity for One Beneficiary	Correspondence	Life Income Gifts	Letter
140	Deferred Gift Annuity for Two Beneficiaries	Correspondence	Life Income Gifts	Letter
141	Pooled Income Fund for One Beneficiary	Correspondence	Life Income Gifts	Letter
142	Pooled Income Fund for Two Beneficiaries	Correspondence	Life Income Gifts	Letter
143	Gift Annuity/Pooled Income Fund Comparison	Correspondence	Life Income Gifts	Letter
144	Life Income Gift	Correspondence	Life Income Gifts	Letter
145	Life Income Follow-Up	Correspondence	Life Income Gifts	Letter
146	Life Income Anniversary	Correspondence	Life Income Gifts	Letter
147	Master Life Income Gift	Correspondence	Life Income Gifts	Letter
148	Accompanying Periodic Distribution	Correspondence	Life Income Gifts	Letter
149	Thank You Letter from Asset Manager to Donor	Correspondence	Life Income Gifts	Letter
150	Describing Real Estate Gifts (Retained Life Estate and Charitable Remainder Unitrust)	Correspondence	Real Estate	Letter
151	Calculating the Charitable Income Tax Deduction for a Release of a Retained Life Estate	Correspondence	Real Estate	Letter
152	General Real Estate	Correspondence	Real Estate	Letter
153	Retained Life Estate	Correspondence	Real Estate	Letter
154	Net Income Unitrust	Correspondence	Real Estate	Letter
155	Charitable Remainder Unitrust for Real Estate	Correspondence	Real Estate	Letter
156	Benefits of a Retained Life Estate and a Charitable Remainder Unitrust	Correspondence	Real Estate	Letter
157	Letter Discussing Benefits of a Retained Life Estate	Correspondence	Real Estate	Letter
158	Presenting Proposal to Donor Explaining Gift of Stock and Tax Benefits	Correspondence	Securities	Letter
159	Describing a Gift Funded with Appreciated Securities	Correspondence	Securities	Letter
160	Describing Benefits of a Deferred Gift Annuity Funded with Stock	Correspondence	Securities	Letter
161	Describing Benefits of Establishing a Charitable Gift Annuity with Appreciated Securities	Correspondence	Securities	Letter
162	Gift of Shares from a Mutual Fund	Correspondence	Securities	Letter
163	Gifts of Securities	Correspondence	Securities	Letter

LIST OF CD-ROM DOCUMENTS *(Continued)*

#	Name of Document	Directory	Subdirectory	Type
164	Gifts of Securities—Stock Transfer	Correspondence	Securities	Letter
165	Gift of Closely Held Stock	Correspondence	Securities	Letter
166	Gift through Life Insurance	Correspondence	Life Insurance	Letter
167	Benefits of a Charitable Remainder Unitrust with a Make-Up Provision	Correspondence	Wills and Trusts	Letter
168	Request for Name in Donor Report	Correspondence	Wills and Trusts	Letter
169	Information on Estate Plan	Correspondence	Wills and Trusts	Letter
170	Substantiation for a Charitable Remainder Trust Gift	Correspondence	Wills and Trusts	Letter
171	Response to Request for Scholarship Information on Including ‹Organization› in Will	Correspondence	Wills and Trusts	Letter
172	Grantor Charitable Lead Trust	Correspondence	Wills and Trusts	Letter
173	Non-Grantor Charitable Lead Trust	Correspondence	Wills and Trusts	Letter
174	Bequest	Correspondence	Wills and Trusts	Letter
175	Explaining the Benefits of a Charitable Remainder Trust	Correspondence	Wills and Trusts	Letter
176	Letter Discussing Trust and Life Insurance	Correspondence	Wills and Trusts	Letter
177	Charitable Remainder Trust and Lead Trust	Correspondence	Wills and Trusts	Letter
178	Confidential Inquiry from Donor's Advisor	Correspondence	Wills and Trusts	Letter
179	Estate Planning	Correspondence	Wills and Trusts	Letter
180	Thank You for Including ‹Organization› in Your Will	Correspondence	Wills and Trusts	Letter
181	To Executor/Attorney of Decedent's Estate	Correspondence	Wills and Trusts	Letter
182	Request for Will	Correspondence	Wills and Trusts	Letter
183	Follow-Up Letter to Executor	Correspondence	Wills and Trusts	Letter
184	Notice to Nonprofit Beneficiary	Correspondence	Wills and Trusts	Letter
185	Thank You Letter/Estate Plan	Correspondence	Wills and Trusts	Letter
186	Marketing Additional Gifts to Unitrusts to Donors and Prospects	Correspondence	Wills and Trusts	Letter
187	The Economic Growth and Tax Relief Reconciliation Act of 2001	Correspondence	Wills and Trusts	Letter
188	Gift of Tangible Personal Property and Calculation of Charitable Income Tax Deduction	Correspondence	Nontraditional Assets	Letter
189	Letter Comparing Endowed and Current-Use Funds	Correspondence	Endowed Funds	Letter

#	Name of Document	Directory	Subdirectory	Type
190	Bequest to Establish a Scholarship	Correspondence	Endowed Funds	Letter
191	Scholarship Transmittal	Correspondence	Endowed Funds	Letter
192	Scholarship, Bequest, Life Income	Correspondence	Endowed Funds	Letter
193	Scholarship, Bequest, Life Income, Real Estate	Correspondence	Endowed Funds	Letter
194	Scholarship, Will, Bequest Request Response	Correspondence	Endowed Funds	Letter
195	Proposal to Convert Current Use to Permanent Endowed Fund	Correspondence	Endowed Funds	Letter
196	Information for Fund Description	Correspondence	Endowed Funds	Letter
197	Update on Endowment Fund Earnings	Correspondence	Endowed Funds	Letter
198	Proposal to Establish Permanent Endowed Fund	Correspondence	Endowed Funds	Letter
199	Ways to Fund a Scholarship with Cash or Stock	Correspondence	Endowed Funds	Letter
200	Memorial Scholarship Agreement Letter	Correspondence	Endowed Funds	Letter
201	Discussing a Major Endowed Fund	Correspondence	Endowed Funds	Letter
202	Thank You Letter from President	Correspondence	Endowed Funds	Letter
203	Endowed Fund Status Report	Correspondence	Endowed Funds	Letter
204	Establishing an Endowment In Honor of Retirement	Correspondence	Endowed Funds	Letter
205	Letter Returning Income to Principal	Correspondence	Endowed Funds	Letter
206	Follow-Up on Request for Information	Correspondence	Follow-Up Letters	Letter
207	Renewing Interest in Additional Gift	Correspondence	Follow-Up Letters	Letter
208	Following-Up Naming Opportunity for a Building	Correspondence	Follow-Up Letters	Letter
209	Prospect Follow-Up—Three Months	Correspondence	Follow-Up Letters	Letter
210	Prospect Follow-Up—One Year	Correspondence	Follow-Up Letters	Letter
211	Donor's Year End Anniversary	Correspondence	Follow-Up Letters	Letter
212	Response to Request from Phonathon	Correspondence	Follow-Up Letters	Letter
213	Follow-Up on Donor's Inquiry	Correspondence	Follow-Up Letters	Letter
214	Letter to Donor at End of Year	Correspondence	Follow-Up Letters	Letter
215	Acknowledgment of Major Gift	Correspondence	Follow-Up Letters	Letter
216	Confidential Inquiry Follow-Up (Use with Document 217)	Correspondence	Follow-Up Letters	Letter
217	Anonymous Donor (Use with Document 216)	Correspondence	Follow-Up Letters	Letter

LIST OF CD-ROM DOCUMENTS *(Continued)*

#	Name of Document	Directory	Subdirectory	Type
218	Follow-Up Meeting to Discuss Charitable Gift Planning	Correspondence	Miscellaneous	Letter
219	Response to Donor Clarifying Role of Organization When Project Is Beyond Scope of Organization	Correspondence	Miscellaneous	Letter
220	Confirming Presentation of Workshop at a Department/ Program at Organization	Correspondence	Miscellaneous	Letter
221	Regarding Naming Opportunity	Correspondence	Miscellaneous	Letter
222	General Inquiry	Correspondence	Miscellaneous	Letter
223	To Inform Program/Department of Gift	Correspondence	Miscellaneous	Letter
224	Outreach to Advisors, Version 1	Correspondence	Miscellaneous	Letter
225	Outreach to Advisors, Version 2	Correspondence	Miscellaneous	Letter
226	To Erect Plaque	Correspondence	Miscellaneous	Letter
227	Letter to Donor Regarding Change of Fiduciary	Correspondence	Miscellaneous	Letter
228	Approval for Publication of Donor's Name	Correspondence	Miscellaneous	Letter
229	Professional Advisory Committee Member	Correspondence	Miscellaneous	Letter
230	Ambassador Program	Correspondence	Miscellaneous	Letter
231	Planned Gift for Class Reunion	Correspondence	Miscellaneous	Letter
232	Matching Gift Information	Correspondence	Miscellaneous	Letter
233	Letter Accompanying Planned Giving Marketing Materials	Correspondence	Miscellaneous	Letter
234	Letter to Disgruntled Donor	Correspondence	Miscellaneous	Letter
235	To Patient	Correspondence	Miscellaneous	Letter
236	Master Combination	Correspondence	Miscellaneous	Letter
237	Thank You Letter	Correspondence	Miscellaneous	Letter
238	Chair Transmittal Letter	Correspondence	Miscellaneous	Letter
239	Assigning Representative of Organization to a Donor's Estate	Correspondence	Miscellaneous	Letter
240	Overview of Planned Gift Types	Administrative Doc	Office Management	Form
241	Planned Giving Donors Detail Spreadsheet	Administrative Doc	Office Management	Form
242	Planned Giving Officer	Administrative Doc	Office Management	Ad
243	Planned Giving Officer Job Description	Administrative Doc	Office Management	Exhibit

#	Name of Document	Directory	Subdirectory	Type
244	List of Questions to Ask a Candidate's References	Administrative Doc	Office Management	Exhibit
245	Planned Giving Assistant: Announcement of Position	Administrative Doc	Office Management	Exhibit
246	Model Standards of Practice for the Charitable Gift Planner	Administrative Doc	Office Management	Form
247	‹Name› Major Gift and Planned Giving Prospect Management Form	Administrative Doc	Office Management	Form
248	Divisional Resource Development Field Report	Administrative Doc	Office Management	Form
249	Divisional Resource Development Field Report	Administrative Doc	Office Management	Form
250	Sheet to Track Performance Goals	Administrative Doc	Office Management	Form
251	Sheet to Track Goals	Administrative Doc	Office Management	Form
252	Planned Giving Baseline Totals	Administrative Doc	Office Management	Form
253	Planned Giving Goals	Administrative Doc	Office Management	Form
254	Planned Giving Office Self-Evaluation	Administrative Doc	Office Management	Form
255	Planned Giving Action Plan for Campaign	Administrative Doc	Office Management	Exhibit
256	Planned Giving Action Plan	Administrative Doc	Office Management	Form
257	Prospect Control Request	Administrative Doc	Office Management	Form
258	Suspect Management	Administrative Doc	Office Management	Form
259	Sample Gift Acceptance Policy 1	Administrative Doc	Office Management	Exhibit
260	Sample Gift Acceptance Policy 2	Administrative Doc	Office Management	Exhibit
261	Management Report Top 100 Donors	Administrative Doc	Office Management	Form
262	Prospect Management Report	Administrative Doc	Office Management	Form
263	Nondevelopment Staff Worksheet to Identify Major Gift Prospects	Administrative Doc	Office Management	Form
264	Checklist to Identify Major and Planned Giving Prospects	Administrative Doc	Office Management	Form
265	Development Inquiries	Administrative Doc	Office Management	Form
266	Donor Contact Report	Administrative Doc	Office Management	Form
267	Event Budget Planning Sheet	Administrative Doc	Office Management	Form
268	Function Checklist	Administrative Doc	Office Management	Form
269	Sample Endowment Questionnaire	Administrative Doc	Office Management	Form
270	Administrative Questionnaire	Administrative Doc	Office Management	Form
271	Gift Administration Form	Administrative Doc	Office Management	Form

LIST OF CD-ROM DOCUMENTS *(Continued)*

#	Name of Document	Directory	Subdirectory	Type
272	Sample Delivery Instructions for Planned Gifts	Administrative Doc	Office Management	Form
273	Bequest File Checklist	Administrative Doc	Office Management	Form
274	Bequest Information Form	Administrative Doc	Office Management	Form
275	Naming Opportunities	Administrative Doc	Office Management	Exhibit
276	Donor Survey	Administrative Doc	Donor Management	Form
277	Worksheet for a Conservation Easement	Administrative Doc	Donor Management	Form
278	Establishing a Scholarship	Administrative Doc	Donor Management	Form
279	Establishing an Endowed Fund	Administrative Doc	Donor Management	Form
280	Prospect Contact	Administrative Doc	Donor Management	Form
281	Donor's Letter of Intent	Administrative Doc	Donor Management	Form
282	Asset Transfer Instructions	Administrative Doc	Donor Management	Form
283	Stock Transfer Instructions	Administrative Doc	Donor Management	Exhibit
284	Donor Intake Questionnaire for Real Estate	Administrative Doc	Donor Management	Form
285	Gift-In-Kind	Administrative Doc	Donor Management	Form
286	Gift-In-Kind—Real Estate	Administrative Doc	Donor Management	Form
287	Donor Intake Questionnaire for Nontraditional Assets	Administrative Doc	Donor Management	Form
288	Donor Intake Questionnaire for Gifts of Oil and Gas	Administrative Doc	Donor Management	Form
289	Gift Annuity Application	Administrative Doc	Donor Management	Form
290	Donor Intake Questionnaire for Real Estate	Administrative Doc	Donor Management	Form
291	Charitable Gift Annuity Administration	Administrative Doc	Donor Management	Form
292	Deferred Gift Annuity Administration	Administrative Doc	Donor Management	Form
293	Pooled Income Fund Administration	Administrative Doc	Donor Management	Form
294	Giving Society Membership Application	Administrative Doc	Donor Management	Form
295	Bequest Distribution	Administrative Doc	Donor Management	Form
296	The Philanthropic Initiative Questionnaire	Administrative Doc	Donor Management	Form
297	Sample Asset Manager's Gift Description and Donor Beneficiary Form	Administrative Doc	Donor Management	Form
298	Know Your Donor Profile	Administrative Doc	Donor Management	Form
299	Planned Giving Stewardship	Administrative Doc	Donor Management	Form

LIST OF CD-ROM DOCUMENTS *(Continued)*

#	Name of Document	Directory	Subdirectory	Type
300	Charitable Remainder Trust Administration	Administrative Doc	Donor Management	Form
301	Bequest Notification	Administrative Doc	Donor Management	Form
302	Tax and PPA Disclosure Charitable Remainder Trusts	Administrative Doc	Donor Management	Form
303	Sample Tax and PPA Disclosure	Administrative Doc	Donor Management	Form
304	Charitable Gift Annuity Processing Packet	Administrative Doc	Donor Management	Form
305	Agenda for Financial Planning Workshop	Exhibits	Agendas	Exhibit
306	Planned Giving Training Program	Exhibits	Workshop/Seminar Materials	Exhibit
307	Planned Giving Training Quiz	Exhibits	Workshop/Seminar Materials	Exhibit
308	Private Foundation, Supporting Organization/ Donor-Advised Fund Table	Exhibits	Workshop/Seminar Materials	Exhibit
309	The Capital Campaign	Exhibits	Workshop/Seminar Materials	Exhibit
310	Development Plan for Nondevelopment Staff	Exhibits	Workshop/Seminar Materials	Exhibit
311	Sample Notice of Probate	Exhibits	Workshop Materials	Exhibit
312	Sample Receipt and Release Form	Exhibits	Workshop Materials	Exhibit
313	Sample Inventory of Donor's Estate	Exhibits	Workshop Materials	Exhibit
314	Notice to Legatee	Exhibits	Workshop Materials	Exhibit
315	Charitable Gift Annuity Annual Income/Charitable Income Tax Deduction for Single Beneficiary for a Gift of $10,000	Exhibits	Charts/Graphs	Exhibit
316	Charitable Gift Annuity Annual Income/Charitable Income Tax Deduction for Two Beneficiaries for a Gift of $10,000	Exhibits	Charts/Graphs	Exhibit
317	Deferred Gift Annuity Annual Income/Charitable Income Tax Deduction for Single Beneficiary for a Gift of $10,000 for a Donor Who Defers Payout to the Future	Exhibits	Charts/Graphs	Exhibit
318	Deferred Gift Annuity Annual Income/Charitable Income Tax Deduction for Two Beneficiaries for a Gift of $10,000 Who Defer Payout to the Future	Exhibits	Charts/Graphs	Exhibit
319	Estate Tax Chart	Exhibits	Charts/Graphs	Exhibit
320	Marginal Income Tax Rate Reductions	Exhibits	Charts/Graphs	Exhibit

#	Name of Document	Directory	Subdirectory	Type
321	Personal Budget and Net Worth Statement	Exhibits	Information to Donors	Exhibit
322	Augmenting Endowed Funds	Exhibits	Information to Donors	Exhibit
323	Sample Revocable Trust	Exhibits	Information to Donors	Exhibit
324	Durable Power of Attorney	Exhibits	Information to Donors	Exhibit
325	Sample Will	Exhibits	Information to Donors	Exhibit
326	Health Care Proxy	Exhibits	Information to Donors	Exhibit
327	Availability and Cost of Long-Term Care	Exhibits	Information to Donors	Exhibit
328	Availability and Cost of Long-Term Care	Exhibits	Information to Donors	Exhibit
329	Facts about Your Long-Term Care Insurance Policy	Exhibits	Information to Donors	Exhibit
330	Personal Information Record	Exhibits	Information to Donors	Exhibit
331	Net Worth Statement	Exhibits	Information to Donors	Exhibit
332	Sample Bequest Language	Exhibits	Information to Donors	Exhibit
333	Master Presentation Inventory	Presentation	Handouts	Presentation
334	Planned Giving: Benefits of Charitable Giving	Presentation	Slides	Presentation
335	Planned Giving: Fund Raising versus Development	Presentation	Slides	Presentation
336	Why Do Donors Give?	Presentation	Slides	Presentation
337	Gift Range Table	Presentation	Slides	Presentation
338	Types of Planned Gifts	Presentation	Slides	Presentation
339	Life Income Gifts	Presentation	Slides	Presentation
340	Charitable Gift Annuities	Presentation	Slides	Presentation
341	Deferred Gift Annuities	Presentation	Slides	Presentation
342	Pooled Income Fund	Presentation	Slides	Presentation
343	Charitable Remainder Trust Options	Presentation	Slides	Presentation
344	Tax Considerations	Presentation	Slides	Presentation
345	Tax Deductibility of Charitable Gifts	Presentation	Slides	Presentation
346	Estate Planning and Charitable Giving	Presentation	Slides	Presentation
347	The Will: A Road Map	Presentation	Slides	Presentation
348	Charitable Provisions	Presentation	Slides	Presentation

#	Name of Document	Directory	Subdirectory	Type
349	Targeting Donors for Bequests	Presentation	Slides	Presentation
350	Coordinating Title to Property with the Estate Plan	Presentation	Slides	Presentation
351	Probate	Presentation	Slides	Presentation
352	Durable Power of Attorney	Presentation	Slides	Presentation
353	Trusts	Presentation	Slides	Presentation
354	The Revocable Inter Vivos Trust (Living Trust)	Presentation	Slides	Presentation
355	Charitable Remainder Trusts	Presentation	Slides	Presentation
356	Benefits of a $100,000 Charitable Remainder Trust Donor Age 70	Presentation	Slides	Presentation
357	Overview of Charitable Remainder Trusts	Presentation	Slides	Presentation
358	Charitable Remainder Trusts	Presentation	Slides	Presentation
359	Asset Classification	Presentation	Slides	Presentation
360	A Gift of Appreciated Securities	Presentation	Slides	Presentation
361	Gifts of Closely Held Stock	Presentation	Slides	Presentation
362	Types of Real Estate	Presentation	Slides	Presentation
363	Overview of Gifts of Real Estate	Presentation	Slides	Presentation
364	Guidelines for Real Estate Gifts	Presentation	Slides	Presentation
365	Considerations in Accepting Gifts of Real Estate	Presentation	Slides	Presentation
366	Gift Options for Real Estate	Presentation	Slides	Presentation
367	Outright Gift of Real Estate or Gift of a Fractional Interest	Presentation	Slides	Presentation
368	Retained Life Estate	Presentation	Slides	Presentation
369	Charitable Remainder Unitrust (Net Income Make-Up Provision)	Presentation	Slides	Presentation
370	Gifts of Tangible Personal Property	Presentation	Slides	Presentation
371	Establishing a Named Endowed Fund	Presentation	Slides	Presentation
372	Establishing a Scholarship	Presentation	Slides	Presentation
373	IRS Revenue Procedure 89-20(1)—Purpose	IRS Forms	Charitable Remainder Unitrust	IRS Tax
374	IRS Revenue Procedure 89-20(2)—Background	IRS Forms	Charitable Remainder Unitrust	IRS Tax
375	IRS Revenue Procedure 89-20(3)—Scope and Objective	IRS Forms	Charitable Remainder Unitrust	IRS Tax
376	IRS Form: Revenue Procedure 89-20—Unitrust	IRS Forms	Charitable Remainder Unitrust	IRS Tax

LIST OF CD-ROM DOCUMENTS *(Continued)*

#	Name of Document	Directory	Subdirectory	Type
377	IRS Revenue Procedure 89-20 (5)—Application	IRS Forms	Charitable Remainder Unitrust	IRS Tax
378	IRS Revenue Procedure 89-20 (6)—Effective Date	IRS Forms	Charitable Remainder Unitrust	IRS Tax
379	IRS Revenue Procedure 89-21 (1)—Purpose	IRS Forms	Charitable Remainder Annuity Trust	IRS Tax
380	IRS Revenue Procedure 89-21 (2)—Background	IRS Forms	Charitable Remainder Annuity Trust	IRS Tax
381	IRS Revenue Procedure 89-21 (3)—Scope and Objective	IRS Forms	Charitable Remainder Annuity Trust	IRS Tax
382	IRS Form: Revenue Procedure 89-21 (4)—Sample Charitable Remainder Annuity Trust	IRS Forms	Charitable Remainder Annuity Trust	IRS Tax
383	IRS Revenue Procedure 89-21 (5)—Application	IRS Forms	Charitable Remainder Annuity Trust	IRS Tax
384	IRS Revenue Procedure 89-21 (6)—Effective Date	IRS Forms	Charitable Remainder Annuity Trust	IRS Tax
385	IRS Revenue Procedure 90-30 (1)—Purpose	IRS Forms	Charitable Remainder Unitrust	IRS Tax
386	IRS Revenue Procedure 90-30 (2)—Background	IRS Forms	Charitable Remainder Unitrust	IRS Tax
387	IRS Revenue Procedure 90-30 (3)—Scope and Objective	IRS Forms	Charitable Remainder Unitrust	IRS Tax
388	IRS Form: Revenue Procedure 90-30 (4)—Sample Inter Vivos Charitable Remainder Unitrust: Two Lives, Consecutive Interest	IRS Forms	Charitable Remainder Unitrust	IRS Tax
389	IRS Form: Revenue Procedure 90-30 (5)—Sample Inter Vivos Charitable Remainder Unitrust: Two Lives, Concurrent and Consecutive Interests	IRS Forms	Charitable Remainder Unitrust	IRS Tax
390	IRS Form: Revenue Procedure 90-30 (6)—Sample Testamentary Charitable Remainder Unitrust: One Life	IRS Forms	Charitable Remainder Unitrust	IRS Tax
391	IRS Form: Revenue Procedure 90-30 (7)—Sample Testamentary Charitable Remainder Unitrust: Two Lives, Consecutive Interests	IRS Forms	Charitable Remainder Unitrust	IRS Tax
392	IRS Form: Revenue Procedure 90-30 (8)—Sample Testamentary Charitable Remainder Unitrust: Two Lives, Concurrent and Consecutive Interests	IRS Forms	Charitable Remainder Unitrust	IRS Tax
393	IRS Revenue Procedure 90-30 (9)—Effects on Other Revenue Procedures	IRS Forms	Charitable Remainder Unitrust	IRS Tax
394	IRS Revenue Procedure 90-30 (10)—Effective Date	IRS Forms	Charitable Remainder Unitrust	IRS Tax
395	IRS Revenue Procedure 90-31 (1)—Purpose	IRS Forms	Charitable Remainder Unitrust	IRS Tax

LIST OF CD-ROM DOCUMENTS *(Continued)*

#	Name of Document	Directory	Subdirectory	Type
396	IRS Revenue Procedure 90-31 (2)—Background	IRS Forms	Charitable Remainder Unitrust	IRS Tax
397	IRS Revenue Procedure 90-31 (3)—Scope and Objective	IRS Forms	Charitable Remainder Unitrust	IRS Tax
398	IRS Form: Revenue Procedure 90-31 (4)—Sample Inter Vivos Charitable Remainder Unitrust: One Life	IRS Forms	Charitable Remainder Unitrust	IRS Tax
399	IRS Form: Revenue Procedure 90-31 (5)—Sample Inter Vivos Charitable Remainder Unitrust: Two Lives, Consecutive Interests	IRS Forms	Charitable Remainder Unitrust	IRS Tax
400	IRS Form: Revenue Procedure 90-31 (6)—Sample Inter Vivos Charitable Remainder Unitrust: Two Lives, Concurrent and Consecutive Interests	IRS Forms	Charitable Remainder Unitrust	IRS Tax
401	IRS Form: Revenue Procedure 90-31 (7)—Sample Testamentary Charitable Remainder Unitrust: One Life	IRS Forms IRS Forms	Charitable Remainder Unitrust	IRS Tax
402	IRS Form: Revenue Procedure 90-31 (8)—Sample Testamentary Charitable Remainder Unitrust: Two Lives, Consecutive Interests	IRS Forms	Charitable Remainder Unitrust	IRS Tax
403	IRS Form: Revenue Procedure 90-31 (9)—Sample Testamentary Charitable Remainder Unitrust: Two Lives, Concurrent and Consecutive Interests	IRS Forms	Charitable Remainder Unitrust	IRS Tax
404	IRS Revenue Procedure 90-31 (10) Effective Date	IRS Forms	Charitable Remainder Unitrust	IRS Tax
405	IRS Revenue Procedure 90-32 (1) Purpose	IRS Forms	Charitable Remainder Annuity Trust	IRS Tax
406	IRS Revenue Procedure 90-32 (2) Background	IRS Forms	Charitable Remainder Annuity Trust	IRS Tax
407	IRS Revenue Procedure 90-32 (3) Scope and Objective	IRS Forms	Charitable Remainder Annuity Trust	IRS Tax
408	IRS Form: Revenue Procedure 90-32 (4) Sample Inter Vivos Charitable Remainder Annuity Trust: Two Lives, Consecutive Interests	IRS Forms	Charitable Remainder Annuity Trust	IRS Tax
409	IRS Form: Revenue Procedure 90-32 (5) Sample Inter Vivos Charitable Remainder Annuity Trust: Two Lives, Consecutive Interests	IRS Forms	Charitable Remainder Annuity Trust	IRS Tax
410	IRS Form: Revenue Procedure 90-32 (6) Sample Testamentary Charitable Remainder Annuity Trust: One Life	IRS Forms	Charitable Remainder Annuity Trust	IRS Tax

LIST OF CD-ROM DOCUMENTS *(Continued)*

#	Name of Document	Directory	Subdirectory	Type
411	IRS Form: Revenue Procedure 90-32 (7)—Sample Testamentary Charitable Remainder Annuity Trust: Two Lives, Consecutive Interests	IRS Forms	Charitable Remainder Annuity Trust	IRS Tax
412	IRS Form: Revenue Procedure 90-32 (8)—Sample Testamentary Charitable Remainder Annuity Trust: Two Lives, Concurrent and Consecutive Interests	IRS Forms	Charitable Remainder Annuity Trust	IRS Tax
413	IRS Revenue Procedure 90-32 (9)—Effects on Other Revenue Procedures	IRS Forms	Charitable Remainder Annuity Trust	IRS Tax
414	IRS Revenue Procedure 90-32 (10)—Effective Date	IRS Forms	Charitable Remainder Annuity Trust	IRS Tax
415	IRS Revenue Ruling 90-103 (Pooled Income Fund; Governing Instruments; Sample Provisions)	IRS Forms	Pooled Income Funds	IRS Tax
416	IRS Revenue Ruling 92-81 (Pooled Income Fund; Governing Instruments; Deductibility)	IRS Forms	Pooled Income Funds	IRS Tax
417	IRS Revenue Procedure 88-53 (1)—Purpose	IRS Forms	Pooled Income Funds	IRS Tax
418	IRS Revenue Procedure 88-53 (2)—Background	IRS Forms	Pooled Income Funds	IRS Tax
419	IRS Revenue Procedure 88-53 (3)—Scope and Objective	IRS Forms	Pooled Income Funds	IRS Tax
420	IRS Form: Revenue Procedure 88-53 (4)—Sample Declaration of Trust	IRS Forms	Pooled Income Funds	IRS Tax
421	IRS Form: Revenue Procedure 88-53 (5)—Sample Instrument of Transfer: One Life	IRS Forms	Pooled Income Funds	IRS Tax
422	IRS Form: Revenue Procedure 88-53 (6)—Sample Instrument of Transfer: Two Lives, Consecutive Interests	IRS Forms	Pooled Income Funds	IRS Tax
423	IRS Form: Revenue Procedure 88-53 (7)—Sample Instrument of Transfer: Two Lives, Concurrent and Consecutive Interests	IRS Forms	Pooled Income Funds	IRS Tax
424	IRS Revenue Procedure 88-53 (8)—Application	IRS Forms	Pooled Income Funds	IRS Tax
425	IRS Revenue Procedure 88-53 (9)—Effective Date	IRS Forms	Pooled Income Funds	IRS Tax

Index

For information about the CD-ROM, see the
About the CD-ROM section on page vii.

John Wiley & Sons, Inc.